CREATE
CONNECTIONS

How to Facilitate Small Groups

RHONDA WILLIAMS
SAMEEN DeBARD
JOSEPH D. WEHRMAN

RESEARCH PRESS
PUBLISHERS

2612 North Mattis Avenue, Champaign, Illinois 61822
800.519.2707 / researchpress.com

RESEARCH PRESS
PUBLISHERS

Copies of this book may be ordered from Research Press
at the address given on the title page.

Composition by Jeff Helgesen
Cover design by McKenzie Wagner, Inc.
Printed by Seaway Printing Co.

ISBN 978-0-87822-721-1
Library of Congress Control Number 2019933778

My dedication of this book goes to all those group facilitators out there, as well as my husband and family. —RW

My heartfelt gratitude to my dear friend, Rhonda Williams, for her guidance and never-ending faith in me. Thank you, also, to the founders of Smart-Girl, Inc., Alma, Debra, Kris and Becky. Additional thanks to my husband, our family, and my parents. —SD

My dedication for this book goes to my wife and three growing kids. Much gratitude to Dr. Grace Ann Mims, as well as the many students I've had the honor to teach. —JW

Contents

Preface

In our combined experience of running hundreds of groups, we have long since discovered our passion for the power and impact of group work. Negotiating our way through the group curriculum and encountering many challenges through our experiences, we have devised an intentional step-by-step process for setting up and facilitating meaningful groups. More importantly, we have found that experiential and interactive groups are much more enjoyable and productive than traditional talk groups. We have also discovered that group activities are inconsequential if an intentional debriefing process is not in place for participants to reflect and apply their learning.

Within any school or community setting, time is often limited when trying to help adolescents, young adults, or professional adults navigate various life obstacles. One-on-one meetings to assist individuals are often time-consuming and have limited impact without consistent and extensive counseling sessions. Small-group interventions provide educators, professional counselors, and community volunteers a time-efficient and effective method for guiding participants through the difficulties of life challenges. Whether in a school or community setting or an advisory or after-school program, small-group activities can have a significant impact on a larger number of members or participants compared to other types of interventions that focus solely on the individual. Why not use our time more effectively and affect more people?

Through small-group interventions, participants are provided with necessary social support while also fostering peer acceptance (Perusse, Goodnough, & Lee, 2009). Research indicates that group-counseling interventions successfully address the social-emotional and behavioral issues of participants (Bailey & Bradbury-Bailey, 2007; Bemak, Chung, & Siroskey-Sabdo, 2005; Paisley & Milsom, 2007; Veach & Gladding, 2007). While groups can address specific behaviors in a meaningful way, they can also provide peer feedback and support in a way that can change lives. Whether through advisory programs or small-group involvement within schools, this type of interaction has been shown to increase attendance, engagement, and practical use of study skills. Adult or adolescent group experiences support bonding, connectedness, and social acceptance in a caring environment. Effectively facilitated groups offer a safe setting in which individuals can practice new skills and work out difficult life situations.

In addition, many people in the business world realize the value of non-cognitive skills such as persistence, resilience, collaboration, and problem-solving in developing successful teams. Businesses demand that their current and future employees be able to communicate well, mediate conflicts, and be productive team players. In the education setting, with the focus on academic success and high-stakes testing, the development of necessary social-emotional and non-cognitive skills is often neglected. This evidence speaks to the demand for the direct teaching of these social and emotional competencies as these needs have escalated at every level of life.

While small-group work is the most time-efficient and functional way of developing non-cognitive competencies, direct instruction in teaching facilitation skills for those leading these groups is also necessary. Intention, purpose, thought, structure, and lesson planning are essential components to initiate a meaningful group experience. Much effort and planning is required of the facilitator in the initial stages of the group process. In an effectively led group, the participants will begin to learn from their experiences, and the facilitator's role shifts to the observation of the process as the participants use their newly acquired behaviors. The participants begin to realize they can lead themselves. The bottom line, however, is that groups are only as effective as the facilitator's skills.

A good facilitator must know the group process with all the ups and downs of group dynamics. A successful group facilitator must also be able to engage the members in meaningful activities, balance the behaviors and dynamics of the members, and help with the application of these newly learned skills in real life. Lacking the skills and competencies to facilitate small groups is often cited as one of the barriers to group implementation. This evidence is an indication that facilitating small groups is not an innate skill. Steps in developing effective facilitation are therefore outlined in these chapters. A successful facilitator can lead experiential activities that simultaneously teach participants useful social coping strategies and self-reflection. If one is not adequately educated and trained in these areas, the interventions will be less beneficial and could even be harmful.

In the beginning chapters of this book, research is presented that supports the effectiveness of using a group process as an intervention strategy. The subsequent chapters introduce group types, and structure and management of group dynamics, which are core components of this book. We will conclude with several curriculum lesson plans. Although there are many small-group lesson plans readily available that utilize the paper/pencil approach to facilitation, the lessons presented in this book are experiential. They allow participants to interact in a dynamic and kinesthetic way, so they are involved in "learning by doing" as opposed to "sitting and getting." These interactive group lessons are in ready-to-use format, so that readers will be able to apply the activities in any group setting.

This book provides the necessary steps to educate teachers, staff, community facilitators, school counselors, social workers, volunteers, and other clinically oriented professionals in the behavioral sciences about meaningful facilitation strategies in teaching social competencies in small-group settings. A successful facilitator is intentional about creating a successful experience for all group members. Small groups have the power to change the thinking, behaviors, and lives of participants if the sessions are well planned and the facilitators have the knowledge and skills to lead effectively. Here is a collection of our knowledge, strategies, and experiences so you can create positive connections in your groups and love them as much as we do!

Acknowledgments

We would like to acknowledge all of the graduate and undergraduate students who have taken the group lab and Adventure Education and Smart-Girl/Guy training courses and workshops. You have certainly taught us as much as we have taught you. Thank you for believing in the magic and power of group counseling.

Our dedication for this book goes to all those group facilitators out there who wanted more practical and applicable information about leading groups. Our hope is that this book will help meet those needs. And to those professionals who are out there leading groups that change the lives of so many: Thank you for your efforts.

Section 1

Group Implementation

1

Introduction

The organic beauty of groups unfolding and blossoming into "life-changing experiences" is the motivation for this book. On numerous occasions, we have been told that our group-facilitation workshops were personally life-altering for the participants. With this consistent reaction, it seemed a natural response to write a book about the process of developing fun, exciting, interactive, and creative groups. Curriculum and activities that we have amassed over the years are only part of the information included here. How to start groups, lead or facilitate groups, and manage group dynamics are all part of the recipe for *Create Connections: How to Facilitate Small Groups.*

The authors share a passion for the collaboration and creativity that are implicit within a group culture. We started with developing social-emotional intelligence groups for adolescent girls and boys, and the excitement that was demonstrated by both participants and facilitators propelled us to develop weekend group counseling workshops for adults. As we observed the adult participants gaining as much insight and self-awareness through the same activities and group processes as the adolescents, we began cultivating cross-generational group training. These experiences elicited similar strong passions and perceptions from the adults as the adolescents. We have applied this same approach in working with active-duty Air Force majors who were selected as commanders for the cadets at the United States Air

Force Academy. Additionally, teaching an annual course in Adventure Education for undergraduate and graduate students and leading community groups have encouraged our creativity and enthusiasm for the group process. Many other participants in our facilitation workshops—including high school students transitioning to college, sixth-grade participants, and high school and middle school teachers—have commented on how engaging in these group activities has shifted their perspectives of themselves. With this validation, it is easy to understand why we chose to share our methods, skills, and curriculum with others, allowing them also to see the value in, and promise of, the group process.

Create Connections

We LOVE groups! Even more than chocolate! While the smooth richness of chocolate may linger for a few seconds, the impact of the group process can remain for a lifetime. Want to Create Connections? This book offers multiple suggestions and ideas about how to develop quality group experiences for all group members as well as facilitators.

Ask yourself these questions: What if you had just lost someone close to you? Who could you talk to about the variety of emotions you are feeling? Your family is going through a divorce, but with whom can you share this difficult circumstance? What if you want to develop good leadership skills? How can you learn to mentor others? Or perhaps it might be helpful if you knew who else you could talk to about the dating violence you are experiencing. What if you just want to talk about girl/guy stuff? The bigger question is where and with whom do you go to discuss any difficult issues? What group of people can you go to in order to connect? Who can get a group started? Who can actually lead a group and make it meaningful?

Small-group support is arguably one of the most powerful, time-efficient, and meaningful ways for people to connect. Unfortunately, there seems to be a shortage of groups that offer real and authentic social and emotional support, experiential education, empowerment, and mentoring or leadership development. There also seems to be a lack of group facilitators who are truly qualified to successfully facilitate groups that encompass these true and authentic aspects.

An often-overlooked component of group process is the intentional debrief that should follow all group activities. The debrief helps group members discuss what was learned during the experience and how to apply it to their lives outside the group: the ultimate purpose of any group. The group is about learning and practicing new behaviors within the small-group setting and then utilizing the new behaviors, thoughts, and attitudes in life outside of the group. Perhaps the most valuable component of this book is its group lesson plans. These lesson plans can be easily and effectively implemented within any group setting, resulting in a creative and innovative group program.

The information and facilitation strategies in this book will support educators, group facilitators, and community organizers—or just about anyone working with groups of people—in developing the necessary facilitation skills, while adding fun activities to their repertoire of resources. This book offers group-facilitation techniques, a skillset often neglected in educational and community training programs. The necessary skills of leading a group with meaning and value are incorporated throughout this book, including social and emotional learning and non-cognitive or essential skills development. This combination can provide personal and professional success in developing powerful groups.

Why Implement Groups?

Small-group interactions are an efficient delivery method for teaching emotional intelligence and non-cognitive (or essential) skills such as self-awareness, communication skills, tenacity, team building, empathy, and cooperation (Farrington, 2012). Group forms of intervention engage adolescents and adults in developing interpersonal relationships in a way that extends beyond what is possible in one-on-one or individual counseling interventions. An educator or youth-program manager who successfully leads a small group of children or adults through a series of experiential lessons can simultaneously teach them useful social coping strategies that equate to practical life skills. This method of learning allows participants to try new behaviors in a safe environment and to develop self-awareness and skills with which to manage life situations and learn more productive social interactions (Campbell & Myrick, 1990).

Directly teaching these non-cognitive skills to adolescents and adults is realized as an effective method in current pedagogy (Conley, 2007; Duckworth et al., 2007; Dweck et al., 2011; Farkas, 2003; Farrington, 2012). Students and adults must be able to communicate well, problem-solve, mediate conflicts, develop personal identities, and be valuable team players to have academic, interpersonal, and professional success. With the focus on academics and testing in schools, these non-cognitive or essential skills are often overlooked in the educational curriculum. However, recent evidence supports how critical it is to teach young people social and emotional intelligence factors, including academic behaviors, attitudes and strategies, and mindsets for their academic and lifelong success (Conley, 2007).

The group process offers more than just an opportunity to "chat" with peers. People "chat" often enough through current social media, texting, and even the occasional direct conversation. When effectively led, the group process offers the disenfranchised adolescent or adult an opportunity to learn productive peer interactions and positive social skills (Perusse, Goodnough, & Lee, 2009). Many people are looking for acceptance, support, and a safe place to express their feelings without judgment. A group that is well facilitated can provide those opportunities for all participants within the group. Interventions incorporated into group activities have demonstrated that student achievement, attendance, and academic work habits are increased

(Steen & Kaffenberger, 2007), and behavioral issues are minimized (Bemak, Chung, & Siroskey-Sabdo, 2005; Campbell & Myrick, 1990).

Knowing that young people and adults often learn better from peers because of shared feelings and experiences, a productive small-group forum can provide that learning opportunity. These types of group interactions are an efficient method of providing a real-life experience in which people can work through difficult issues and simultaneously provide peer support for others (Perusse, Goodnough, & Lee, 2009).

Increased self-efficacy, better anger management, and diminished social anxiety have resulted from small-group experiences (DeRosier, 2004). Additionally, social competencies and personal awareness are developed, and inter- and intrapersonal relationships enhanced, through small-group sessions (Bemak, Chung, & Siroskey-Sabdo, 2005, p. 378). This mode of teaching and support has demonstrated enhancement of achievement scores, more positive personal relationships, and responsible behaviors (Bemak et al., 2005; Campbell & Myrick, 1990; Shechtman et al., 1997). May and Housley (1996) indicate that group counseling was more successful than individual counseling with sexually abused young people and at-risk youth. Bemak, Chung, and Siroskey-Sabdo (2005) demonstrate that young people gained better social competencies and social-skills development when group members brought unique insights and perceptions to small-group discussions.

Additional benefits from the group experience include peer mentoring (Rosen & Bezold, 1996) and collective problem-solving that enhance inter- and intrapersonal skills. Social issues and developmental difficulties can also be addressed in small-group settings. Topics such as dating-violence prevention, blended families, cultural awareness, multicultural responsiveness, social justice issues, social and emotional intelligence, and leadership can also create change in oneself and others when addressed through this modality.

As Malekoff (2004) states, "Group work is one avenue for promoting the reflection and critical thinking necessary to clarify values and make healthy decisions" (p. 6). He supports group work as a method of teaching critical-thinking skills and enhancing group members' personal, social, physical, and intellectual boundaries, forcing healthier ways of self-expression.

Group work allows individuals to commune, commiserate, and collaborate in a safe and structured environment. Malekoff (2004) views group work as a place to find belonging, hope, self-confidence, and competence, where individuals are not defined by their deficits but their strengths. Groups can provide a caring, nurturing, and safe space in which one can practice new behaviors and beliefs without judgment.

This time-efficient delivery method can have valuable and immediate personal impact on the maximum number of participants (Bemak et al., 2005). Groups are arguably one of the most productive methods for managing the serious social issues that people bring to schools, after-school programs, or work settings. Despite the issues present, groups can be incredibly fun with plenty of smiles, laughter, and bonding among members.

People commonly assume that creating, developing, and implementing a group is an easy task of simply convening a collection of like-minded individuals together. Rather than haphazard group development, we suggest a structured, intentional, and purposeful group selection and process. This book aims to help make the group-development process both enjoyable and productive. The more one front-loads the planning process, the easier it will be to create connections in your groups.

2

Group Types

Group types, like zebra stripes, can vary widely in format and intent! Therefore, an important consideration for intentional group development is group type. Numerous factors should be considered when initiating a group and determining its type. The Association for Specialists in Group Work (ASGW) identifies four fundamental group types: task groups, psychoeducational groups, counseling groups, and psychotherapy groups (Thomas & Pender, 2008). This book addresses primarily psychoeducational and counseling groups. The advantages and disadvantages of heterogeneous and homogeneous groups will be explored in the following chapter along with suggestions regarding implementing an open versus a closed group. Virtues of gendered groups, depending on the developmental stages/ages of members and the intent of the group, will also be discussed. All these group-type decisions must be made prior to beginning group member selection.

Categories of Groups

While this book focuses primarily on psychoeducational and counseling groups, we feel it is important to briefly describe the other two types of groups. Of the four types of groups, task groups are the simplest to explain.

As the name implies, these are groups established to achieve a specific goal. The focus of a task group is less about personal growth or self-awareness, as the accomplishment of the goal is the priority for the participants. It is not the intention of this book to cover task-group development or facilitation skills.

Psychotherapy groups are considered emotionally in-depth and longer-term groups. They commonly explore personally problematic issues shared by or common among members. These types of groups intend to develop self-awareness and coping skills regarding a specific and challenging life issue. Members' personal issues tend to be severe in nature, and the focus is to create behavioral and thought-processing changes at a deep emotional level through the efforts of personality reconstruction (Erford, 2011). Like task groups, the intent of this book is not to cover psychotherapy-group development or facilitation skills.

Create Connections: How to Facilitate Small Groups concentrates on psychoeducational and counseling groups and will explore, in detail, group facilitator skills, member dynamics, and thought-provoking initiatives within the included lesson plans. According to Nina Brown (2009), psychoeducational groups place value on both dissemination of information and exploration of feelings. The group facilitator blends observations of the affect or feelings of members with delivering cognitive material in a developmentally appropriate and engaging manner.

Psychoeducational Groups

Psychoeducational groups use a flexible approach that centers on constructs such as personal development, empowerment, prevention, and support through life transitions including family and caregiver support, to name a few (Brown, 2009). This type of group is commonly structured to emphasize skill development through experiential activities and initiatives. Interventions offer members a chance to empathize with other group members, while also identifying unacknowledged similarities (Brown, 2009).

Psychoeducational groups provide an opportunity for participants to verbalize and emote regarding commonalities among them, creating a safe environment that can enhance quality of life. Brown (2009) suggests that "this type of group allows for the intensity of the feelings to be lessened and can even reduce the possibility of uncontrolled expression, thus teaching self-management skills" (p. 222). Valuable components of psychoeducational groups include flexibility of the topics and format, and a focus on prevention, intervention, and/or personal growth.

The group facilitator typically defines the activities and structure, while "presenting group members with the opportunity to learn new information and skills, draw connections to previous knowledge, and make personal meaning of the information" (Bryan, Steen, & Day-Vines, 2016, p. 208). Psychoeducational groups allow facilitators to meet the needs of more individuals in a more direct and time-efficient manner. They are convenient and functional for a small or large number of participants, and the direction of the group can shift, allowing flexibility to meet members' needs. There is, however, a fine line, cautioned by Nina Brown (2009), between presenting sufficient information and allowing the group process to grow organically in which self-disclosure and self-awareness are encouraged. Examples of psychoeducational groups include leadership, peer counseling, social skills development, or gendered groups. These may be heterogeneous or homogeneous groups in their structure, a topic that will be discussed later in this chapter.

Counseling Groups

The focus of working on interpersonal issues through self-disclosure is an example of counseling groups as defined by the ASGW (Rapin & Keel,

2007). These groups tend to be problem-centered and remedial in nature, yet encourage self-growth and behavioral change: "... students explore issues affecting their development, and experience acceptance and support from their peers, while exploring various problems and increase coping skills" (Southern et al., 2010, p. 9). Compared to psychoeducational groups, counseling groups tend to be smaller in the number of participants and shorter in the duration of group time. They are typically homogeneous in nature, as the group members have experienced similar issues. This type of group is discussed at length later in this chapter. Examples of counseling groups include grief and loss, divorce, blended families, or military deployment groups. Anger management or friendship groups can be considered either counseling or psychoeducational groups.

The type of group that a facilitator chooses to initiate is an important first consideration based on the goals and intentions of the group. Is it your intention to teach skills through experiential initiatives and activities to allow the participants to develop personal awareness while also sharing feelings and insights? If this is the case, you are likely looking at a psychoeducational-group format. Do you intend to combine participants with a shared personal issue in order to discuss, self-disclose, and process the emotions surrounding that particular issue? If so, you are likely to initiate a counseling-group format. While the two group types can be interchanged, the group may be most effective if the facilitator is intentional in the decision about which type of group to develop.

Heterogeneous Versus Homogeneous Groups

The next informed decisions a facilitator should consider when they use *Create Connections* are whether to create a heterogeneous or homogeneous group and if the group should be open or closed. These decisions will impact the members' experiences, so being intentional and informed in these decisions is critical to group success. As Irvin Yalom (1985) states, "The composition of a group makes a substantial difference and influences many aspects of group function" (Adler, 1995, p. 270).

A heterogeneous group is a collaboration of diverse individuals with a variety of life experiences. There is no one common issue; instead, the group is broad in topics and focused on activities and initiatives. It is important to consider that in a heterogeneous group the facilitator will need to work hard in the early sessions to build strong cohesion and trust among members. As cohesion can be more challenging to develop in heterogeneous groups, it is crucial for the facilitator to develop trust and connectedness, while at the same time balancing any conflicts that may result from a lack of group cohesion.

A homogeneous group, on the other hand, tends to be problem or issue focused, with all group members having experienced the same issue or problem. Michal Adler (1995) defines the homogeneous group as having a clearly defined focus or goal, using the terms *common problem* and *case-centered*. This type of group can incorporate different levels of homogeneity such as age, specific life experience, or gender (p. 15). Lieberman (1990) indicates that homogeneous groups are "a unique set of individuals who share a common dilemma, and it is from them that help can be derived" (p. 32), with group cohesiveness being the priority for success. The jury is still out regarding the most efficient group type: heterogeneous or homogeneous. Despite the research, one is not necessarily better than the other. The decision about group type should factor into the group's intent and goals.

In terms of the strengths of each type, Glaser (2004) advocates for the creativity of heterogeneous groups. This author adheres to the heterogeneous concept, finding it to have less redundancy and more innovation. Change is more likely to occur within a heterogeneous group, according to Adler (1995), as it allows for the creation of a social microcosm or "adaptive discomfort," which is necessary for change to occur. A diverse and broad range of experiences is shared within the group, which leads to cultivating varieties and depth of ideas. Because of the diversity of views in a heterogeneous group, this group type may impact a larger number of its membership. As participants mentor each other, the members expand their resources.

Heterogeneous groups can enhance social learning and manage conflict (Hess, 2007). Additionally, research supports the value of cognitive frameworks and reframing through a heterogeneous group as opposed to just "feeling" an experience, which might occur within a homogeneous group (Hess, 2007; Lieberman, 1990).

On the other hand, Powell (1990) suggests that the level of trust and solidarity in a homogeneous group allows members to sustain the interpersonal connections for longer periods of time. According to Lieberman (1990), group cohesiveness is the priority for success in a homogeneous group. The second condition is providing "a setting that is different from ordinary social interaction" (p. 32). Homogeneous groups develop a "specific articulated ideology, as a set of beliefs for defining the nature of the common problem" (Antze, 1979). While this can feel supportive in a group setting, it can also be limiting when trying to have members develop a full range of options, strategies, and resources that might be available to overcome the common or shared problem.

Another core tenet of *Create Connections* is the ability to see the problem from different points of view or multiple perspectives. Homogenous groups may imply that only individuals who have been through the same problem can relate to each other. Thus, a drawback to homogeneous groups is the development of "group think" and a lack of alternative strategies and problem-solving. The homogeneous group can limit the discussions to only the identified "problem topic," disallowing exploration of other confounding issues (Lieberman, 1990). The cohesiveness, while most palatable within a group, can also serve as a protection from the harder work of challenging each other's perceptions. Because the group members in a homogeneous group feel so connected to each other, they often will not risk challenging a peer within the group for fear of losing the cohesion and connectedness.

The authors of *Create Connections: How to Facilitate Small Groups* utilize heterogeneous groups most often. Throughout the many groups we have facilitated, the similarities of the group members, identified through activities, help connect the group, while the differences enhance the growth of the group. The valuable peer-mentoring between members and the diverse perspectives add worth to the group experience. However, our experience has taught us that much time must be spent in developing trust and cohesion within the group from the beginning, before pushing forward to more challenging and taxing activities and topics that could cause group dissonance. By manifesting group cohesion from the start, most "adaptive discomfort" or conflict is much more manageable and productive because the connectedness still exists. Ultimately, no matter the type of group that is employed, it is essential to explain the intent and objectives of the group and what the group process looks like from the beginning. Likewise, it is just as important to clarify whether the group will be closed or open, a topic that will be explored next.

Closed Groups Versus Open Groups

Whether the group will be a closed or open is a critical decision that must be made before group implementation. A closed group typically has a fixed membership and is time-limited and theme-oriented (Wilson, 2010). Advantages of a closed group include knowing what to expect from week to week from members and facilitators. While group cohesion will be a primary focus in the initial stages of the group, trust between group members won't have to be continually revisited because new members will not be added. There is no guesswork about how a new individual will impact the group dynamic since new members are not added as the group continues.

Additionally, the ebb and flow of the group process will not be as dramatic because the group maintains the same members throughout its existence. The continuity of the lessons and the integrity of the group can add stability and continuity. However, some of the drawbacks for closed groups are the lack of novelty within the group. Group members can become complacent and stagnant in their thinking and problem-solving strategies. Facilitators must maintain vigilance in monitoring co-dependency issues or other group dynamics that might occur when no new members, hence no new experiences, are introduced.

Suggestions for effective management of a closed group will necessitate that a guideline or rule regarding attendance is put in place early so all participants will understand its value and importance. A fresh and engaging activity for each group meeting will keep the group moving forward. It will be important to monitor and manage the group dynamics, so there are no negative repercussions from the closed group such as negative members' interactions or stagnant thinking.

On the other hand, an open group brings with it a different set of advantages and disadvantages. An open group can collect or repopulate the group with new members (Brown, 2009). A new group member may stimulate new conversations and interactions within the group, which can change the group dynamics for the positive, allowing members to see a new point of view. Disadvantages of an open group might include the effect of a new person on group dynamics. The group may regress instead of progress (Wilson, 2010, in Erford). Establishing group trust and cohesion must be an ongoing process in open groups, and lack of consistency with members' attendance will make assessing group effectiveness more difficult.

Suggestions for open groups include pre-screening each new group member and pre-planning how to include new group members into the system. Nina Brown (2009) suggests that the group members be notified before a new individual joins them. A discussion about the feelings of the inclusion of a new group member may help pave the way for a more successful transition. Encourage members to empathize about how the new member might feel about coming into the group, and brainstorm ways to include the new member. Wilson (2010) encourages the group leaders to "have a small set of clearly articulated goals for the group as a whole in order to provide focus for the group and the keep the scope of the group…" (pp. 89–90).

Some leaders leave their groups open because they fear attrition within the group. Attrition in and of itself is not a sufficient reason for keeping a group open. A closed or open group decision should be pre-planned, and not a reactive response to members leaving the group. If attrition is occurring within the group, a careful evaluation of how the group activities and processes are going may be helpful. Reflection on the curriculum used, group structure instituted, interconnections of group members, or even an assessment of one's own facilitation skills may be necessary to reignite a flailing group. The authors encourage keeping the group open for two, maybe three weeks for new members, but then to close the group in order to maintain consistency and cohesion. This strategy establishes a group's willingness to be inclusive of others, but after three sessions the group will have developed its own culture, and adding new individuals may be more detrimental to the group than maintaining the current membership.

Gendered Groups

One last consideration for group types is the use of gendered groups. This decision should be made based on the goals of the group, the developmental age of the members, and the intended curriculum to be used. Having gendered groups may enhance the effectiveness of the activities and may add value to the group process. Adolescent groups, in particular, may benefit from gender-specific groups. Researchers (Clewell et al., cited in Bell and Norwood, 2007) found that "to be effective, interventions must be grounded in an understanding of the growth and developmental needs of students...as well as a sound knowledge of educational experiences" (p. 249). The physical and emotional changes taking place among participants in this age group tend to influence decision-making, social interactions, and critical thinking. LeCroy and Daley (2001) agree that cognitive capacities impact sociocultural experiences. Since male and female brains develop differently, at different times and in different ways (Sax, 2005), it may be beneficial to teach coping skills and social strategies that are sensitive to needs of a particular gender. "Effective program development occurs when gender differences and gender strengths are an inclusive part of the curriculum" (Williams & Ferber, 2008).

If facilitators are working with adolescents, it is important to remember that self-esteem can be very fragile, especially for girls at this age (LeCroy & Daley, 2001). By utilizing gender-specific groups, a safe space to explore personal identity and social relationships is offered. Girls are more likely to talk about female issues with a group of girls, while this topic would not be as likely in a mixed-gender group. Although the authors have encouraged heterogeneous grouping in the previous section, there is an advantage in considering gender-specific groups when dealing with developmental issues such as personal identity and social relationships, particularly with adolescents.

Intentional consideration of group types—including heterogeneous or homogeneous membership, closed or open group structure, or gendered or mixed membership—will establish the groundwork for the next layer of group development. These important structural decisions provide a foundation for group effectiveness. The more considerations that are contemplated on the front end of group implementation, the more time the facilitator and group will have to enjoy its interactions. Weighing the options carefully can set up the group for success!

3

Ethics for Great Groups

The number of people involved in a group process increases the number of ethical issues that can arise within the group. This caution is not intended to cause fear in the hearts of group facilitators. It is, however, a message to encourage group leaders to be conscientious, aware, and knowledgeable about the issues that could come up. The cliché "Forewarned is forearmed" is very apropos when working with groups.

This chapter is a guide for group leaders/facilitators regarding ethical concerns that could arise when working with groups. There are many ethical issues that can occur in a group. However, they can be circumvented by having a meaningful plan for the group, and by following professional ethical guidelines.

A facilitator must consider how to screen group members and create an informed consent. Ethical consideration must be given to how the limitations of confidentiality will be discussed within the group setting. Group-facilitator competencies, cultural awareness, and sensitivity to the diverse members of the group are also part of ethical practice. Understanding ethical issues as group leaders is an invaluable skill that can protect the group members and group facilitator. While it is the intent of this chapter to draw attention to a few of the significant areas of ethical concern, more intensive research on this subject should be part of an effective facilitator's training. This section is only an introduction to ethical considerations in group work, and it is not intended to be comprehensive. This chapter offers a few general suggestions regarding responses to members, ethical resources, and reactions to ethical concerns.

Group Screening

Thorough and purposeful group-member screening procedures can help cull potential ethical issues that may arise in a group. Ethical guidelines of the American Counselor Association (ACA) and American School Counselor Association (ASCA) declare the importance of screening candidates before they are invited into the group. Assessing the suitability and level of commitment of each participant is the precursor to having a productive group (Stone, 2013). Further impetus for screening group members is based on the ASCA Ethical Standards for School Counselors (American School Counselor Association, 2010, sec. A.6.a), which states "The school counselor [group facilitator] takes reasonable precaution to protect members from physical or psychological harm resulting from interaction within the group." These precautions come from the effort of screening group members.

Vetting potential members allows for expansion of the purpose of the group while also gathering information about the participant and evaluating their appropriateness. Understanding the context from which the prospective group member comes is invaluable for the facilitator in predicting attitudes, behaviors, and motivations for being in the group (Association for Specialists in Group Work, 2000). Screening questions could include: How well does the potential group member work with others? Is the individual capable of understanding the information and purpose of the group? Are the goals of the group compatible with the individual? For example, when screening youth for group membership, "not all students necessarily benefit from small-group process, as their social skills may not be up for the challenge of group dynamics" (Kolbert, Williams, Morgan, Crothers, & Hughes, 2016). The group-member screening process can include informed consent at the same time as the interview, a process that will be discussed next.

Informed Consent

Best practice in group work includes an informed consent for all potential members. The process of informed consent not only protects the rights of the individuals but also provides information about what the participant will be doing in the group and outlines expectations of members. The consent form allows potential members to make an informed decision for voluntarily committing to the group process.

Informed consent includes:

- Defining the boundaries of the group

- Clarifying the nature of the group relationship

- Sharing goals of the group

- Identifying risks and benefits of the group

- Explaining time, cost, logistics

- Defining limits of confidentiality and mandatory reporting (Corey, Corey, Callanan, & Russell, 2004).

Informed consent must be given in a manner that is understandable for every participant. The informed consent process should be ongoing throughout the duration of the group. It is therefore vital to consider the age and level of comprehension of each participant. When introducing informed consent, the developmental capacity of the members must be taken into consideration, which raises the issue of how young people give informed consent. Children and adolescents need to be informed about what the group experience might entail. With underage participants, parents will need to be informed as well as sign a consent form. The American Counseling Association Code of Ethics (Section B, 2010) reinforces the value of "developing a collaborative relationship and respecting the parents' rights to help their child." Thus, if the facilitator is practicing ethical protocol, not only should child or adolescent group members be informed but parents/guardians too. Helping group participants understand the group process benefits all and lays the groundwork for transparency and trust.

Confidentiality

While confidentiality is the cornerstone of trust within a group, it is a double-edged sword as well. Understanding the complexity of confidentiality is crucial for productive and ethical group facilitation. Confidentiality is maintained by the participants within the group. A *Create Connections* facilitator will set the tone and the expectations for confidentiality upfront, early and ongoing, within the group. However, it is impossible to guarantee that confidentiality will be maintained within a group setting.

The Guidelines for Group Psychotherapy Practice, from the American Group Psychotherapy Association (AGPA), state that a group facilitator "is knowledgeable about the limits of privileged communication as they apply to group therapy and informs group members of those limits." The American Counseling Association Code of Ethics (ACA) dictates, "In group work, counselors clearly explain the importance and parameters of confidentiality for the specific group" (American Counseling Association, 2016, sec. B.4.a). The ASCA Ethical Standards for School Counselors agrees with the need to "communicate the aspiration of confidentiality as a group norm while recognizing and working from the protective posture that confidentiality for minors in schools cannot be guaranteed" (American School Counseling Association, 2016, sec. A.7.e).

The necessity of addressing confidentiality within the group is made clear in the ethical statements mentioned above. It is vital to help group members understand the importance of confidentiality within the group. Members should also understand the repercussions of breaking confidentiality and the value of trust within the group.

The other edge of the sword, however, is the importance of describing why a group facilitator may be legally obligated to break confidentiality. The limits of confidentiality have legal as well as ethical implications. In defining the limits of confidentiality, the terminology we commonly use to describe boundaries is the "three *H*s": harm to self, harm to others, and being harmed. Simply repeating these phrases does not constitute an adequate explanation of what they mean. For comprehensive informed consent, it is important to break down each of the phrases so that each participant understands the meaning. In elaborating on each of the three *H*s, the facilitator must consider the ages and the capacity of understanding of each of the participants within the group. For example, a group of adults discussing examples of harm to self might include drinking and driving, taking illicit drugs, or self-mutilation. These examples will present differently with a group of sixth-grade girls, and therefore it is important to understand that the meaning of the three *H*s will vary depending on the age and capacity of the group members. The facilitator's description should be very intentional.

Being harmed must be clearly defined because of its many implications. Group facilitators are considered mandated reporters in most states, and a participant's disclosure of being harmed in any way, no matter the age, may constitute a mandated report to the appropriate entities. Although younger students may feel that being bullied is being harmed, it may not necessarily qualify depending on the scenario and the regulations of the environment in which the groups are occurring. On the other hand, a young person who is being harmed by an adult in a position of trust requires an immediate facilitator response as a mandated reporter. There are many implications to consider with a disclosure of being harmed.

The third "*H*," harm to others, constitutes a threat to another person and may also require reporting by the facilitator. Every state, every school district, every community organization has specific requirements about how to handle of this type of report. It is therefore incumbent upon the facilitator to know the state laws regarding the limits to confidentiality, mandatory reporting policies, and the protocol of the organization in which the group is occurring when making a report.

Another aspect of confidentiality limitations is the facilitator's competency in handling a disclosure of harm within the group. For example, when a group member discloses something that falls under mandatory reporting requirements, it often becomes a focus and concern for all group members. At the point of such a disclosure, the facilitator must take control of the discussion. It would be inappropriate to have an extensive discussion with all group members about a potential legal issue with one person, as it could impair a possible investigation. On the other hand, a facilitator does not want to seem unsupportive of the group or the member who has disclosed. Best practice is to notify everyone in the group that the facilitator will work with the individual to handle this in the most appropriate way. Reinforcing that the disclosure will be dealt with by group facilitator can be reassuring for all group members. Often it is a relief for the members to know that someone else will carefully handle this important information and will help the individual who has disclosed. However, it is imperative to reiterate the need for confidentiality from all group members to ensure a supportive and respectful response to a participant's experience.

While in the beginning stages of the group, it is important to present the "three *H*s," and doing so is essential to help group members understand the value of maintaining confidentiality. When working with youth, the group leader must also address confidentiality and parent or caregiver interest in knowing what happens within the group sessions. Over the years of leading groups, we have at times received comments from adolescents such as, "My mom wants to know everything I am doing" or "I can't keep secrets from my parents." It is important for group leaders to support the parents' right to know what is happening with their child in group sessions.

Typically, in response to these types of statements, we encourage the participants to share, with their parents or caregivers, the activities that we do in the group or any of the lessons learned from the group experiences. However, we also try to clarify that when it comes to sharing another group member's personal stories or experiences with someone outside of the group, that crosses the lines of, and breaks, confidentiality. It is important to let group members know that if it is not their personal story, then they do not have the right to share it outside of the group. A "no gossip" guideline can be an opportunity to develop positive social skills at any age. This can lead to a discussion about betrayal by friends, which usually helps younger participants understand the value of trust. The facilitator should help the group members set boundaries about confidentiality, giving them a sense of safety and security, which is one of the pinnacles for effective facilitation.

Facilitator Competencies

Another topic related to ethics is the group leader's competency and training. Research in *School Counseling Principles: Ethics and Law* (Stone, 2013) indicated that 79 percent of school counselors felt competent or very competent in leading small groups. While it is good to know that the majority of these professionals feel positive about their skills, it is also important to note that every professional organization supporting group facilitators—whether ACA, ASCA, AGPA, or ASGW—has ethical standards of practice. All of these organizations expect a facilitator to work within the boundaries of their professional competence. Additionally, it is compulsory for group facilitators to seek ongoing training in the group process and skills. The *ASCA Ethical Standards for School Counselors* (2016) encourage specialized training when dealing with difficult topics such as incest, eating disorders, trauma, or self-mutilation. It is ethically incumbent upon the facilitator to be trained in the areas in which they are practicing. These competencies, which abide by professional ethical standards, protect group members as well as group leaders. An additional area of facilitator competency that is often overlooked is cultural awareness, which will be discussed next.

Cultural Awareness

The unique experiences, personalities, and backgrounds of individuals and their interactions in a group setting affect the way the group operates. Understanding that these differences and similarities exist and knowing how they can affect group development is crucial to leading a group successfully (Williams, Lantz, & Noorulamin, 2008, p. 14). Each group member brings the many parts of who they are to the group, and the intersections of race, ethnicity, gender identity, and able-bodied add a new flavor to the interactions and impacts the richness of the experiences.

It is vital that facilitators appreciate differences while celebrating similarities among group members. Failure to acknowledge the importance and impact of culture and other significant intersections could lead to ethical challenges. Ethical expectations mandate that group leaders become aware of personal biases regarding race, ethnicity, gender, class, culture, sexual identity, etc., through ongoing education. The ASCA Ethical Standards for School Counselors (American School Counselor Association, 2010, sec. A.10.a), encourage facilitators to strive to create a safe, respectful, nondiscriminatory environment that demonstrates respect and civility toward all. Additionally, the ASGW Best Practices in Group Work Guidelines (Association for Specialists in Group Work, 2007, Sec. B.8) explicitly states, under the heading "Diversity": "Group Workers practice with broad sensitivity to client differences including but not limited to ethnic, gender, religious, sexual, psychological maturity, economic class, family history, physical characteristics or limitations, and geographic location. Group Workers continuously seek information regarding the cultural issues of the diverse population with whom they are working both by interaction with participants and from using outside resources."

Understanding the value of culture for group members contributes to the inclusivity of all participants. In this type of environment, members can thrive and flourish in the trust that is built.

Ethical Decision-Making

To navigate complex ethical dilemmas that arise in the group setting, it is imperative for group leaders to operate from a defined ethical decision-making model. With the many professional organizations that support group facilitators, it is invaluable to find a useable ethical decision-making model. For example, one commonly used by school counselors is Carolyn Stone's Solutions to Ethical Problems in Schools, or STEPS (Stone, 2013):

- Define the problem emotionally and intellectually

- Apply the ASCA Ethical Standards for School Counselors

- Consider the students' chronological and developmental levels

- Consider the setting, parental rights, and minors' rights

- Apply the ethical principles of beneficence, autonomy, nonmaleficence, loyalty, and justice

- Determine potential courses of action and their consequences

- Evaluate the selected action

- Consult

- Implement the course of action (ASCA Ethical Standards for School Counselors, 2016, sec. F).

4

Group Structure and Group Dynamics

Create a Safe Space

Of all the tasks and topics surrounding the growth of *Create Connections* groups' implementation, the pinnacle focus is on creating a safe group space. No matter the lesson plans, the group-member selection process, or the best intentions, if the facilitator doesn't spend time developing safety within the group, the success of the group experience will be challenging. Although safety within a group is often not explicitly addressed in group-development books, it is key to the success of any group setting. This topic is commonly overlooked because facilitators assume every group member wants a safe place, and will therefore intuitively know how to establish one. However, when members come from a wide variety of life experiences and challenges, they may not be able to clearly identify or know how to create a safe environment. Addressing safety explicitly so there are no assumptions about what it means to participate in a safe group is essential. When we refer to safety within a group, it is about physical as well as psychological security. An informed facilitator will intentionally factor in both areas of safety for every activity and discussion topic introduced.

Considerations for physical safety include the soundness and stability of the equipment used. An example might consist of plywood boards being passed from one participant to another in the communication puzzle initiative. Is there a chance of splinters in passing the board, or that lifting the board in such a way could cause another member to get hit with it? There are many tag games in the curriculum included in this book. Creating a safe area for everyone to run is vital. If participants are running or chasing each other as in the Rock/Paper/Scissors tag, the facilitator must think about whether the current space is adequate for the activity or whether there is another area outside that might work better. Typically, few activities should require lifting. However, if lifting a participant is a possible strategy to solve an initiative, facilitators should ensure that group members know how to lift with their legs, not their backs, if lifting is an option. A rule of thumb we often use is that no one can be lifted higher than the group members' hips. So, a piggyback ride might work, but raising someone higher than that becomes too much of a physical risk and not worth an injury.

An additional consideration for physical safety is the inclusion of any members with a physical challenge. With prior planning, any activity can be differentiated to accommodate those with physical differences. Part of creating a physical and emotional safe space is that ALL members are included in ALL activities. It is helpful to have a variety of appropriate and inclusive accommodations in one's back pocket, so they can be utilized when including others who are physically challenged. Although there is a myriad of safety considerations beyond what is discussed in this chapter, it is the facilitator's responsibility to monitor the group's physical and emotional safety at all times.

Creating an emotionally secure environment is another critical factor in group success. No participant wants to walk into a group and question if they are going to be ridiculed or negatively judged. An effective facilitator will ensure that every member feels that their ideas are heard and respected.

They should know that under no circumstances will bullying behaviors be tolerated. Based on the parameters developed in the guidelines activity, as well as the behaviors of the facilitator, participants should be assured that the group will be collaborative, cooperative, and inclusive of all members.

A safe environment is generated first by the modeling of the facilitator. Safety is created from the moment the group members enter the group for the first time. This type of environment is established through group discussion and activities, including a warm welcoming of individuals at the initial group meeting. Safety can be reinforced in the creation of the group guidelines. Using a reflective question—such as "How do we make this group a safe space?"—allows group members to consider what they want from the experience and have influence in the creation of the safe space. Further, having participants brainstorm words that describe their ideal group environment, as well as those conditions that establish comfort and safety, will be more powerful since it involves all members of the group in this process. Simply telling participants what they should do to create a safe space lacks the opportunity to provide them empowerment and ownership in the process. Words such as *respectful, collaborative, fun, friendly*, or *caring* may come from the group members as they brainstorm how they want the group to feel. From there, as the development of group guidelines, norms, and promises take place in the second or next sessions, these words developed by group members can be revisited, utilized, and incorporated.

We find it effective to use the first group session to preview activities and topics participants will experience in future sessions, and the second sessions to establish group guidelines. When leading groups, we value creating a fun and valuable experience in the first session so group members want to return for the next session. As developing group guidelines (never referred to as "rules" because of the negative associations that may be present with that word) is a significant component of developing a safe environment, it will be essential to consider the timing of the introduction of this topic. Please note that developing the group guidelines is an activity that is explained in the curriculum portion of this book (on p. 68).

It is also helpful to keep in mind that a facilitator asks questions rather than gives answers. "As a facilitator, the role is about managing the interactions, not giving the answers or directing the group... An effective group facilitator gives the power back to the group and allows the group to practice the lifelong skills of problem-solving and risk-taking [in a safe environment]" (Kolbert et al., 2016, p. 146).

Managing Disruptive Behaviors

Entire books have been written on the subject of group behavior management, and whole educational courses are dedicated to this topic. The limited suggestions in this book regarding behavior management for group members should be supplemented with other behavior management resources that are currently available. Based on our numerous group leader experiences, working with very young children to adults, we have found a few tried and true practical responses that we find valuable to share in this chapter.

In responding to group behaviors, the first tenet of effective management is to keep the focus on the group as a whole, not the individual's distracting behaviors. A common pitfall in group management is to call out a particular child by name. A group facilitator should focus on the behavior, not labeling a group member. Reprimanding one group member in front of the group can be very shaming and may cause that person to become the "identified patient" within the group. This kind of reactivity may also cause other group members to feel unsafe. In counseling, the identified patient is typically synonymous with group scapegoat. If one of the group members is identified as a "problem" in the group, the facilitator must manage the fallout that comes with labeling. The repercussions could manifest in other members being mean or making fun of the group member. The members might isolate or taunt the identified member. It could result in reinforcing the negative behaviors of the identified group member and possibly members' judgement of that individual. Above all, it exacerbates the feelings of shaming, exclusivity, and being in an unsafe environment—all opposites of a safe space.

Effective methods of group management generalize the disruptive behaviors as opposed to reprimanding one member in front of others. A discussion about appropriate group behaviors could be helpful. It might begin with something such as, "Hey, team, I am noticing some things that are happening in the group that make me feel uncomfortable. What kinds of behaviors are happening? What would make our group better?" Another approach might be, "Team, what do we try to focus on in this group?" One hopes that the answer will be group safety or teamwork. This discussion allows the facilitator an opportunity to ask about which negative behaviors might cause the group to be unsuccessful and which behaviors might be more successful. By reflecting on effective and ineffective behaviors, members can choose for themselves how to act. Another technique might be to reiterate the group norms that were created by everyone. The facilitator might ask, "Are the group norms being followed in this activity, or do we need to talk about them some more?"

Power Plays

When working with difficult group members, it is important to consider what the person who is acting out is trying to gain. Commonly, the answer is power. In such a case, the facilitator may be able to subtly give a participant some power without disrupting the entire group. Ideas such as assigning the disruptive member a task or a leadership position may help redirect the behavior. In other words, disrupt the disruptor. An example of such an intervention might be to give the individual the power to be the only one who can talk, or perhaps after all the members have shared their problem-solving ideas, the problematic member might be allowed the leadership skill of making the final decision. By giving power to a member, the facilitator is also giving them a chance to practice new, positive behaviors. Facilitators should always consider what the acting-out participant needs from the group that they may not be getting. Considering this can help the facilitator redirect the negativity and hone better coping skills for all group members.

Attention-seeking behaviors are about getting the group to pay attention. And for some participants, negative attention is better than no attention. While we advocate for giving the group a chance to self-correct, there are occasions when the negative behaviors may require a more direct intervention such as a one-on-one conversation. If a one-on-one intervention is necessary to help manage a behavior, it will be important to have the discussion when all of the other group members are distracted by another task. This may be done during a bathroom break, a snack time, or a time when the group is transitioning to another activity. It remains important not to publicly humiliate an individual. The subtler the intervention, the better chance you have of keeping the safety of the group intact. There are many specific types of behaviors that can be distracting to group success. A few are mentioned below with intervention suggestions.

Naysayer: The name certainly speaks to the behavior. Being around someone who is incessantly negative and rarely has anything positive to say can be exhausting. In addition, this behavior can rub off on other members of the group unless an adequate response is given. One generalized method of mitigating this behavior is to have a discussion and an activity about useful leadership skills. Which is more effective: positive, supportive leadership or negative, authoritative leadership? This discussion might help the naysayer realize the impact that negativity can have on the group. If such a behavior exists within the group, it might be useful to revisit the guidelines that were created by the group. Ask reflective questions such as, "Are we having fun? If not, how do we create a more fun group?" or "How do negative comments take away the fun or trust that we have developed in this group?"

Another strategy for handling this behavior is to have positive members speak about what they liked about the activity before allowing a negative person to speak. This intentional structuring might help dispel some of the negative comments if all of the members see that most everyone else had a good time. A stronger response may be required if the derogatory behavior doesn't change, however. Reminding all group members that attendance is voluntary may encourage behavior redirection. If someone is choosing to leave the group, they owe it to their peers to explain why they have made such a choice. Putting the responsibility back on the person who is creating the negative atmosphere is an important facilitator strategy.

Quiet/shy participant: Some participants may be very introverted. Perhaps they have never been given a place to voice their ideas or thoughts or may not know how to speak up for themselves. Thus, it may not be helpful for the facilitator to force the quiet person to speak. It may only reinforce the anxiety of speaking up. However, strategies may be created by the facilitator to help with this behavior. One suggestion is to hand out two or three pipe cleaners. Every time someone speaks through the group process, they must put one pipe cleaner in the middle of the circle. Additionally, all pipe cleaners must be used before we move to the next activity. This strategy encourages all of the group members to self-monitor their speaking. Not only does it promote the quiet member to speak, but it also supports the over-talker to measure the number of their comments.

The "round strategy" can also help with managing over- or under-talkers. With forewarning that each person will be expected to share a thought about their experience, the group members are informed that everyone will be asked to speak. This notification allows everyone to be more intentional about what they share. One caution we would include here is the "right to pass." While a member might choose the right to pass when a discussion is occurring, we suggest limited use of that privilege. As facilitators, we have found that the right to pass can be misused and overused. Allowing for passes can be used as a passive/aggressive maneuver. It might elicit a method of silent protest: "I don't like this topic or where it is going." Although the right to pass may actually be an authentic request, it opens the door for being used inappropriately.

A suggestion: if a member asks for a "right to pass," the facilitator can immediately create a boundary around that option. For example, "Indeed you can pass for now. We will come back to you when everyone else has shared." Setting up the expectation that you will come back to that person allows them a chance to consider their answer while also being held accountable for a response. When given safe boundaries and opportunity, the quiet individual usually finds their voice and wants to be an active member of the group.

Group clown: Usually this behavior by a group member has been slowly developed over their lifespan. This behavior is often seeking power or creates a distraction if the topic is uncomfortable for that participant. Whatever the reason behind the behavior, it can be frustrating to have in a group setting. As the facilitator, you certainly don't want to dampen the creativity of an aspiring comedian; however, learning that there is a time and place for humor may be a helpful life lesson for the group member. Again, a strategy of group discussion regarding positive leadership may be beneficial.

It is worth a discussion about how safety of the group may be impaired if someone is clowning around. It is incumbent upon the facilitator to stop an activity if the group is not physically or emotionally safe. One other strategy might include pulling the "clown" aside at an appropriate time to talk about the distracting behavior. The facilitator can honor how funny they might find this participant but encourage the jokester to think about when it is okay to joke and when it is not okay. Clowning around can also be contagious and minimize the impact of the activities in which the members are engaged.

Cliques within the group: As is true of all of the disruptive behaviors that have been mentioned, exclusionary cliques can cause a lot of complications within a small group. While you might think this behavior occurs only in adolescent girl groups, you would be wrong. This behavior happens with college classes and adult interactions as well. It is quite natural for people of any age to begin to create a stronger connection with a smaller subset within the group. This behavior may enhance a sense of safety for this smaller group of participants, but it can also limit interactions and opportunities to create connections beyond this smaller group.

If allowed to continue in the group setting, clique behavior can undoubtedly create a power imbalance among participants, minimize the effectiveness of the facilitator, and create hurt feelings. Once again, this is a distraction that can be mitigated by making sure an inclusion statement is in the group guidelines. Referring back to the group guidelines may help in managing the exclusionary behaviors. However, an intentional approach by the facilitator may be the most effective. It is always the job of the facilitator to create an inclusive, accepting group environment. From the beginning of the group, such intentional strategies as mixing pairs of members for each activity help to create an inclusive, not exclusive, group culture.

We have found it best to not allow group members to "group" themselves. We attempt to be unpredictable in how we group members. The more unpredictable the facilitator is with moving group members around, the more likely they are to keep factions from forming. Plan ahead regarding how to challenge the group to sit next to someone new each time it meets. For example: Sit next to someone with the same colored shoes as yours. Line up according to your birthday (then the facilitator divides the groups). Assign the groups based on three favorite foods, and point to each group member and say, "You are pizza, you are nachos, you are candy."

Be creative in adjusting where group members sit or with whom they interact. If group members know they will continuously move around, the facilitator can manage clique behavior more effectively. When the group norm is that the members are always moving and interacting with each other, cliques become a mute issue. This constant regrouping creates a culture of acceptance and inclusion, which is a valuable life skill all ages and group members can utilize.

Other Group Management Strategies

Rounds: There are many reasons to use rounds. This strategy allows each group member to comment or reflect on the experience or process. A major reason a facilitator may use rounds is to give everyone a voice within the group. It becomes an expectation that every member will reflect on every activity. The facilitator can preface the round by saying something such as, "Give me one feeling word that you have about this experience or give one sentence about how this was for you." As previously mentioned, rounds help manage the over-talker and offers the under-talker more of a chance to think. Rounds can also allow a great time-management technique. To maximize the benefit, don't do an activity if you can't debrief it. However, if you find you are running short on time, rounds can be a shortcut for the debrief. Asking group members to share one word or one sentence about how they will apply their learning from this activity gives participants a chance to reflect. Lastly, the round is an excellent way to complete a discussion and transition to the next activity.

Frontloading: Simply stated, this technique is used to forewarn a group ahead of time of behaviors that might interfere with the productivity of the activity. An example might be: "Today we are going to talk about sexual harassment. I know this group is mature, and they can handle the discussion without giggling or being silly about this very serious topic. Mature groups have good questions and a great discussion. I hope I can count on you to handle this." This approach prepares the group for the expected behavior.

No one wants to be identified as immature, so negative behavior is avoided. Another area where the facilitator might consider frontloading is an activity where body size could be a concern. Additionally, for any activity that requires physical or emotional safety, it is good to "frontload" in a gentle and caring manner.

Talking sticks: This strategy is an invaluable tool to use in managing any group. Young or adult groups benefit from having some constraints on those who blurt out or talk over others during a discussion. A talking stick can be any type of object that is held by the group members when they are talking. It is then passed to the next participant who wants to speak. As long as a person holds the talking stick, no one else can interrupt. We suggest using an object that does not cause a distraction in and of itself. Often a stuffed animal works and can be the group mascot. If the talking stick is introduced early in the group sessions, it becomes the group norm. We caution that it can be disruptive to introduce it in later groups, as participants may realize its introduction is to manage one member's over-talking. This could identify an individual instead of making the talking stick a group norm.

Freeze frame: While this technique should be used infrequently, it can be necessary when there is a group safety issue. A facilitator can call "FREEZE" at any time an activity is not going well. Used sparingly, it can have the necessary effect of momentarily stopping an activity so participants can process what is currently happening in the group. It can allow team members time to reconsider or restructure their strategies. It can also be used as a time for the participants to adjust inappropriate behaviors. While this intervention can be useful, it is not a platform for the facilitator to necessarily admonish the group.

Additionally, the freeze frame should be used with a question: for example, "Okay, I need everyone to stop for a moment. FREEZE. Look around you. Are all of the team members participating equally? If not, what can you do as a group to change that, so everyone is involved?" This is a quick intervention. Allow the group to self-correct. A facilitator should not have to tell the group why they were asked to freeze. Allow the group to consider their own actions. Facilitators ask questions of the group rather than tell the group how to be. They help the group reconsider perceptions and actions, just as in a reframe.

Reframing: During a group session, the facilitator may often observe that the group is headed in a negative direction. This can be an opportunity for the facilitator to reframe a comment or perception. Reframing simply means that the facilitator questions the group perception and suggests another way to look at the situation. If, for example, a group fails at a task, the facilitator can reframe the "failure" as a chance to learn from what didn't work and have a do-over. Reframing something helps participants reconsider a negative point of view and helps members develop a growth mindset.

Fishbowl: Another group management strategy is the fishbowl. On occasion, it is helpful for participants to get feedback, or allow new leaders to step up. This technique is where one or two participants, or even half of the group, watch as the other members engage in an activity. The fishbowl can be created with any number of observers for any number of purposes. If the facilitator wants to challenge some members to take on the leadership role, those observers may be designated as the only participants who can talk. This strategy is helpful when differentiating an activity for someone in the group with a physical challenge so they can be the group talker even if they cannot physically interact. The fishbowl gives members a chance to give and receive feedback. While it is important for the facilitator to teach and model for members how to give and receive feedback, the fishbowl also helps participants to accept and incorporate new information about themselves or their behavior.

There are many more strategies that can be added to this list for effective group facilitation. In this section, we have presented a few suggestions on how to manage challenging situations that may arise. Negative group behaviors can derail a group, cause conflict within the group, and most certainly challenge the facilitator's skills. A facilitator cannot afford to be so reactive that everything becomes a problem, and it is essential to pick and choose carefully the issues to which they react. Heavy-handed or punitive responses can shut a group down, however, having no response gives unspoken permission for members to act out inappropriately. Learning the balance between some reaction and allowing the group to move forward at its own pace is key to success. Remember that group connections are created from the group's experiences.

5

Group Development and Debriefing Strategies

As illustrated thus far in this book, effective groups do not lead themselves. A facilitator considers several things to direct the group toward productive learning. Some considerations to ensure a successful group experience for all members include: What are the ages of the group members? Are they developmentally in about the same range? How should I adjust the curriculum to meet the developmental needs of these participants? How do I structure the group to minimize any possible issues or concerns? How do I make the debrief of every activity meaningful for the participants? These questions and more will be answered in this chapter, so you too can *"Create Connections."*

Ages and Stages

Regardless of their ages, group members want to know what the group procedures will be at the onset of the group. They want to know what to expect, and yet at the same time, they want to be inspired to come to the group anticipating some new type of learning. If the structure is not predictable, and the activities and discussions are not stimulating, the members may not attend.

However, facilitators must factor in that developmentally what engages a sixth-grader looks a lot different from what engages an adult. Considering these factors will help group leaders develop a positive and fun group experience for all members. While we will not be discussing the specific details of every developmental age and stage throughout the lifespan, this chapter will focus on a few points for consideration.

Attention spans tend to equate with the number of birthdays one has had. If group members are six years old, the facilitator can expect to have their attention for about six minutes, but even the oldest participants have a limited ability to focus for more than 12–15 minutes. So, lesson planning requires a transition or topic shift based on the typical length of the members' attention spans.

Developmental components of group structure also need to be considered in planning a group session. Younger students require more structure. However, the middle school and high school–age participants need some boundaries around different areas such as bathroom breaks and use of cell phones during sessions. Depending on the behaviors and the group dynamics, more structure may need to be implemented as the group evolves. We suggest starting the group with a stronger structure and adapting as the group matures.

The elementary-grade participants rely on adults to have control and management skills, so they have a safe group. Many young children will therefore acquiesce to the adult decisions. If the facilitator comes unprepared to a group meeting, a message of not being important is sent to participants of any age. Members perceive that they are not worth the time of the facilitator, which can challenge the effectiveness of the facilitator.

Not only is the developmental level of the group members of critical importance, but their coping skills and emotional management skills are also a consideration for a facilitator. Appropriate behavior modeling for younger group members is helpful, as they are learning social and emotional management. On the other hand, older students are just beginning to practice a new range of emotional management and developmental skills. That is why modeling is also so powerful for middle and high school students. Adult participants may require more direct processing using "caring confrontation" to help them glean more effective behaviors.

Stages of a Group

While it is essential to factor in the developmental ages of each of the group members, it is equally important to consider the stages of the group dynamics as a whole. This additional aspect of a facilitator's awareness is necessary to bear in mind, as it can determine the success or failure of a planned activity. Although the developmental stages of group dynamics do not always flow in a linear path, knowing the stage of the group will be helpful in planning appropriate activities and thoughtfully debriefing discussions. Forming, Norming, Storming, Performing, and Mourning (Tuckman & Jensen, 1977) are descriptors of group development that are easy to remember. However, a variety of other models for group development are available for consideration. As a group facilitator, consider which activities, interventions, and discussions will be most helpful in each of these stages. We will assume at this point that the screening and invitation for participation have already been completed. The next step in group dynamics is about getting everyone together on the same page and forming the group.

Forming: This stage includes the initial introduction of members, the rationale of the creation of the group, general logistical information, explaining the structure and process of the group, and developing a group name. All of the participants will be busy checking each other out and making judgments about the other participants. It is normal for the participants to feel anxious, excited, and curious. To accommodate this mixture of feelings, it will there-fore be essential for group members to have some fun through interactive and engaging activities in the beginning stage. This will help the participants avoid some of their anxiety about the group process. The more engagement and fun that occurs in the first group, the more likely the participants will be to return with positive anticipation.

The most important part of the forming stage is developing group cohe-sion. Low-risk "getting to know you" activities will help the group move through the suspicious and skeptical perceptions of each other that can occur during this stage. Previously in this book, we suggested that devel-oping group norms in the first session is not a good strategy. Establishing group norms, or guidelines, are not necessarily a high-energy activity. Thus, a facilitator might leave the development of the group norms for the second session. Make the creation of these guidelines fun and engaging!

Norming: Creating a warm, welcoming environment every time members walk into the group is a key to developing a trusting culture. If the facilita-tor is still putting items out or preparing activities and not greeting mem-bers when they walk in the door, the anticipation and anxiety will continue to build within each member. It is also helpful if every member has a task as they walk in the door. Some "sponge activity," in which members can draw a picture of their week, or having participants collectively draw on a "Whatever Board," are suggestions as participants enter the group. Writing down words that describe their mood can be a method to get them centered and focused on the group environment. At the same time, this sponge time allows for other members to enter without peer judgment. Activities at the forming stage may still be low risk, but the initiatives should soon progress into a deeper level of sharing. Remember that the more group members laugh and have fun, the less likely they will be to discount each other or con-tinue to be reserved.

Storming: This group developmental stage is where group members begin to challenge and confront each other and/or the group facilitator. This stage often causes fear in the hearts of facilitators. Often facilitators can hinder a group from the storming phase because of their own personal fear of conflict. Storming happens in every group at some point. While it can be uncomfortable for the facilitator and the participants, keep in mind that part of the group process is to learn how to handle life experiences productively. Group members who can learn to resolve conflict effectively will develop some invaluable life skills. The facilitator's job at this point is to use their attentive listening and empathic skills while remaining neutral. Rephrasing comments, reflecting feelings, and helping group members hear feedback from their peers in the group are all vital skills in a mediation process. Normalizing feelings and allowing group members to realize the impact of their own words can provide powerful learning opportunities. The trick is not to take any anger or dissension personally.

As a facilitator, it is essential to help group members to express frustration in a way that moves the group forward. Activities during this stage are likely to be more intense. Helping group members develop a proactive voice and identify personal needs is an excellent learning opportunity, especially during times of conflict. Although facilitators may try to be mind readers, we cannot always predict when a conflict or challenge will occur. It can be helpful to have standby interventions available when this storming or conflict occurs. Remember, people seldom have the opportunity to see conflict handled productively.

Performing: As is typical with any conflict, redefining and repairing relationships within the group so that group productivity can continue is a significant task in reforming the group process. At this stage, group members learn to approach challenges more effectively. They learn to collaborate and connect better and can give feedback to each other that is helpful rather than hurtful. Sometimes members' most significant learning is the difference between passive, aggressive, and assertive behaviors. During the performing stage, the essence of small-group experience emerges. At this point in group development, the members may no longer need the facilitator to intercede as much. This verifies that the group is capable of speaking with their own voice, asking for what they need and solving their own challenges or problems.

Although it is not unusual for a group to regress to storming at some point during the sessions, an effective facilitator will merely reinforce the coping skills the members have acquired. Allowing the group to utilize their new skills will add to the cohesion of the group and the development of lifelong strategies. The performing stage is also an excellent time to review the personal and group goals that were established in the initial stages of the group process. This review may help members refocus on their original intentions and help them utilize their newly developed communication skills.

Mourning: Also referred to as adjourning, this stage is the closing or completion of the group. Mourning or adjourning can be a very moving and emotional time for group members. Some group members may be angry about leaving, since it could be the only caring and connected experience they have had. Others may be ready to move on. However, no matter each participant's feelings about group closure, it will be an essential time to review their goal achievements (or lack of achievement). Reflecting on group accomplishments and identifying the new strategies that each person has developed will be valuable to revisit as well.

Most importantly, the final session should be unique and honoring. The facilitator must be very intentional with the closing activities so every member can feel connected and special. Like conflict and other intense feelings that may have arisen in the group process, closure is a normal part of life.

Teaching group participants how to close a chapter of their lives gracefully is yet another invaluable life skill. Make it memorable for the group members. Within every group, there will be a need to address individual developmental needs and differentiate the activities to include all group members.

Debriefing Activities

Many group facilitators initially assume that facilitating a group requires minimal effort and training. Asking questions should not be difficult, since we do it all the time. What could go wrong in a debrief when I am just asking questions about their experience? Unfortunately, many novice facilitators fail to realize the value and importance of a structured format when debriefing an activity. By structuring this part of the session, the debrief helps participants to focus on the experience they have just had, reflect on how they engaged in the activity, and contemplate what the experience means to them and their future behaviors. If the facilitator expects that participants will make meaning out of the experience on their own, then the facilitator is not doing their job. Making meaning is a guided thought process. It helps participants process the event they just experienced so they can apply the new information to their own behaviors.

If you do not have time to process an activity, then, in our opinion as facilitators of group connections, it is best not to conduct the activity, or at minimum to adjust your goals regarding what is to be achieved in this group experience. Although activities can be fun and entertaining, that perspective alone is missing the point of having activities in the curriculum. The groups that you are growing are about social, emotional, and personal growth. Leaving out the debrief or processing can diminish the value of the group. Random questioning is not an effective method of processing an activity. At the beginning of developing your processing skills, do not rely only on your thoughts or observations about the group's interactions and behavior during the activity. Instead, write down several questions before and perhaps during the performance of the activity. There is no shame in writing down thoughts as a debrief progresses.

The most straightforward format for debriefing an activity is to utilize three question forms: *What, So What,* and *Now What.* These questions were developed by some of the gurus in experiential education such as Karl Rohnke and John Luckner. This process makes debriefing easier to follow and allows for more reflection from group members.

- The **WHAT** questions are immediate responses to the activity. What just happened? What did we just do? What was that experience like for you? Although the questions do not have to start with the word *What,* this type of probing gives the facilitator a chance to hear how the activity was perceived and how the group interactions occurred. This tends to be the most extended portion of the debrief, as all of the members usually want to share how they experienced the activity.

  In this part of the debrief, managing the excitement of telling individual stories may be a significant part of behavior management. The facilitator will not just ask one question from each of the question forms but will listen attentively to what the group members are saying. Reflective statements can lead the group to further discussion about the immediate experience: "It was hard for your group to make a decision about how to solve this problem" or "So, some of your ideas were not heard." If time allows, the facilitator can allow the group to stay in the immediacy of this reflective moment until all sharing is complete.

- **SO WHAT** is the next level of debriefing. This is about the purpose of the activity. Such questions might include, "Why do you think we did this activity?" "What was the purpose of this?" "What was the point?"

Although this section is not as lengthy as the first section, it can evoke some new thoughts about the experience. If there has been conflict in the activity, this may be the time when the participants project anger onto the facilitator. It is important not to take the projection personally, as members are trying to make sense out of the experience. If the activity did not go the way the team thought it would go, then being angry is a natural response. It is now the facilitator's job to model for the members how to handle frustration and help them question their own responses. This portion of the debrief also allows the participants a chance to see the intention of the activity.

- **NOW WHAT** is the final portion of the questions and is about the application of the learning from the activity to group members' lives. It allows for making meaning out of the experience. This is when the facilitator helps the group begin to identify what they learned about themselves and the functioning of the group. Deeper meaning and personal insights require that the facilitator be very present and focused during this portion of the debrief.

In this questioning, the facilitator can individualize learning for each group member. For example, one group member may have identified a personal goal of speaking up more often or another may have difficulty with over-talking in a group. Pinpointing each member's goals, or the behavior changes they had previously identified, gives them time to self-reflect and consider behaviors they might apply from this new learning to their daily lives. Depending on the cognitive level of the group, this can be a lengthy discussion, or if time is running short, it may be just one question: "What are you taking away from this experience?" In this case, be sure that every member of the group can voice their response. Thus, the "Rounds" technique is used here as was described earlier. This section can also be used as the summary of the activity. The participants can address what they have learned about themselves or, if another activity follows, it can be used to consider changing how the group is working together.

As you will see, there are suggestions for debriefing the activities in the following curriculum or develop your own. Feel free to use the debrief questions included in the curriculum. With practice, you will develop your style of questioning. The *What, So What, Now What* questions give you a format to follow. No matter how many times you run an activity, the reactions and responses will be as different as the members of the group. Having a format will help keep you focused and directed toward a learning purpose.

In the next section, a series of curriculum activities are provided. Please feel free to use these with your groups. The progression of these activities is intentional, moving from low-risk to more in-depth topics. The beginning initiatives are fun, light, "get to know you" activities commonly used during the forming stage of the group. Following them are activities that provoke more thought and response from group members. The final section's activities are less intense in terms of topic and more focused on closing the group during the mourning/adjourning stages of the group process. We hope you have fun with these activities!

Section 2

Curriculum and Activities

How to Use This Curriculum

The following small-group curriculum activities have been developed and organized to be implemented sequentially within a small group or an advisory setting; however, the individual activities may be utilized in any order that the facilitator sees fit, in order to best meet the specific needs of the audience. It is important to always consider the developmental needs of the group as the facilitator selects activities.

Activity Format and Delivery

All activities, regardless of the order in which they are delivered, should follow the outline/process below:

- **Introduction:** Use a creative method to engage or "hook" participants while also gently introducing the topic or activity. This can be done through creating a metaphor, sharing a brief story, asking the group a question, doing a role-play, etc.

- **Facilitate the Activity:** Provide all necessary instructions and details so that participants have a clear understanding of the mission and what they are being asked to do. "Chunk" and simplify the information while including any safety parameters and limitations prior to beginning the activity. Interject when necessary with further clarification, guidance, or support while not trying to rescue or micromanage the activity.

- **Debrief:** At the conclusion of each activity, allow the group to process the experience, reflect on individual learning, and discuss group challenges and growth. As was previously explained in chapter 5, debriefing questions can best be formatted in the *What*, *So What*, and *Now What* framework.

Examples of debriefing questions are listed below:

"What" questions allow for immediate reflection on what just took place:

1. What did we just do?

2. What was that like for you?

3. How did it feel to participate?

4. Where did you struggle?

5. What helped you succeed?

"So What" questions are to ask about the purpose of the activity:

1. What do you think was the purpose of this?

2. Why did we do this activity?

3. What was all of this for?

"Now What" questions allow participants to apply the experience and learning to their own lives:

1. How does this apply to you?

2. How does this relate to school/work/your family?

3. What are you going to do differently next time?

4. What is one thing you learned that you can use in the future?

5. Who else can you use this with or teach it to?

Check-In & Check-Out

A "check-in" is conducted at the beginning of each group meeting, in which every person briefly responds to one or two questions of the day, in a circle/round. This process helps the group come together, focus their energy, and disengage from life outside of the group for a little while. The check-in also allows group members and the facilitator an opportunity to gauge the tone of the group and assess any individual needs. Similarly, a "check-out" is done at the end of each meeting to reflect and provide closure to the day.

It is important to have a consistent scaling question during each check-in and check-out in order to assess what level or mood everyone is at, from one to ten (one being the lowest and ten being the highest). In addition to the scaling question for each session, a second check-in question is creative and intended to help the group members focus on the identified topic each session. An example for a group session on friendships might include the check-in question "What is one quality you want in a good friendship?" Using the same premise, the check-out question might then include the scaling question paired with "Can you name one way you are a good friend?"

Additional Sample Check-In Questions

To be used in addition to the standard scaling question "What level are you on, from one to ten?"

1. If you could live a day as any celebrity, who would it be and why?

2. What is your "get-pumped" (energizer) song?

3. What kind of a first impression do you think you make?

4. What is the most interesting thing you have ever eaten?

5. What is your favorite smell?

6. How would you describe your dream car?

7. Name one item in your bedroom that has special meaning to you. Why is it special?

8. If you could create any app for your phone, what would it be and why?

9. Whose face do you look forward to seeing every day?

10. If you could relive one day over and over again, what would it be and why?

11. What moment in your life has made you proud of yourself?

12. Who is one person who stands out in your memory?

13. What's an important piece of advice you've been given?

14. If you had to eat one food for an entire week, what would it be and why?

15. Netflix or movie theater?

16. What's your favorite family tradition that you hope to continue?

17. What is one example in your life of how you've been brave?

18. What is the craziest thing you want to achieve in your lifetime?

19. Order in or eat at a restaurant?

20. How has the education you've received so far impacted your life?

21. What's a way you have seen kindness affect someone?

22. If you could go back and change one thing from high school, what would you change?

23. What are you most looking forward to in the next five years?

24. If you could do a duet with any artist, who would it be and to what song?

25. What is one thing you've done that you didn't think you could do?

Sample Check-Out Questions:

To be used in addition to the standard scaling question "What level are you on, from one to ten?"

1. What was your favorite part of today?

2. What did you enjoy most during our time together?

3. In one word, how would you describe today's experience?

4. What's your take-away from today?

5. Fill in the blank: "I'm surprised that _____."

6. Fill in the blank: "I learned that _____."

7. Fill in the blank: "I am excited that _____."

8. What did you connect most with?

9. Based on today, what is one thing you will do before we meet next time?

10. What did you learn about yourself?

11. What new thought/idea did you get out of today?

12. How was today different from previous groups?

13. What have you learned for next time?

14. What are two ways that you will implement the lessons from this session into your life?

ACTIVITY: SHARE AND TRADE

Objective

To engage in low-risk conversations as a method to both share and receive information about oneself and others.

Materials

Four Starburst candies per person. If you prefer not to use candy, you could use differently colored Post-its or pipe cleaners instead.

Introduction

Ask someone in the group what their favorite flavor of Starburst is and then also share what yours is as well. Then say, "Even though my favorite is strawberry, I enjoy having the other options of lemon, cherry, and orange too for a bit of variety."

Directions

Give each group member four Starbursts of the same color. Each person, however, should have a different color group. For example, one person will have four yellow candies; another will have four oranges, etc. The group will have three minutes to exchange their candies, one at a time, so that they end up with one of each color by the end (pink, orange, yellow, and red). In order to trade candies, one must walk around and engage in conversation by asking another group member a question about themselves such as, "Where did you grow up?" or "What is your favorite time of day?" Once both partners have asked and answered a question, they can then trade one candy each in an effort to help one another get one step closer to reaching the goal.

Depending on time, stop the activity once the first person has a complete pile with one candy of each color. Otherwise, allow the activity to continue until a few more participants have exchanged candies.

Debrief

1. What did we just do?

2. What were your conversations like?

3. How did you feel when you walked in today?

4. How do you feel now, after having mingled a bit?

5. What is something you learned?

6. What did you notice about yourself as you engaged in conversation?

7. What role do you typically play in groups?

8. How did this process build comfort in our group?

9. What was the purpose of this activity?

10. How does it relate to you as a person?

ACTIVITY: NAME GAME

Objective

To learn names in a creative, fun manner while also encouraging participants to take a risk and share a bit of their personality with the group.

Materials

None.

Introduction

Share a personal example of a time when your name was mispronounced or when you called someone else the wrong name. Briefly discuss how you felt/reacted in that situation. Another option is to ask if everyone is able to name all other members of the group. Since it is unlikely that anyone will be able to do so, this further builds the need for such an activity.

Directions

Have the participants stand in a circle as they think about the first letter of their first name. Once in position, ask them to think of a positive, non-physical adjective that starts with the same letter as the first letter of their first name

Adapted from Williams, R. L., Lantz, A. E., and Noorulamin, S. (2008). *Making Smart Choices: Social and Emotional Skills for Adolescent Girls.* Alexandria, VA: American School Counselor Association.

(i.e., Smart Sammy). Lastly, have them add a physical motion/action to complete this combination. For example, Sammy might point her finger to her head while saying, "I'm Smart-Sammy." The rest of the group then repeats her adjective, her name, while also pointing their finger to their own head to mimic the same words and actions as Sammy.

The person to Sammy's left then says his adjective, name, and does his action. The entire group repeats the second person's adjective, name, and action and then rewinds back to Sammy to repeat her name combination as well. This pattern continues in a clockwise rotation until all group members have introduced themselves, while also going back each time to repeat all previous name sequences.

If the group learns the names very quickly or if there is extra time, do an additional round in which you challenge them to go through all of the names again, as fast as possible. Or, ask for a volunteer to close their eyes and do a round all by themselves. Make sure the volunteer has a lot of positive encouragement and recognition for having the courage to try it on their own.

Debrief

1. What did you enjoy about that process?

2. Why did we learn names in this manner rather than just putting on name tags?

3. What aspects of this activity might have been uncomfortable for you?

4. What surprised you?

5. Why is it important to learn and remember names?

6. What did we learn about each other in addition to our names?

7. How did the adjectives and movements help us remember names better?

8. How does it feel when someone remembers your name and pronounces it correctly?

9. What was the purpose of this?

10. How can you apply this to the future?

ACTIVITY: SOMEONE LIKE ME

Objective

To make connections with others, explore similarities, and celebrate differences.

Materials

One chair per person, minus one. Tape or paper can also work as place markers.

Introduction

Ask the group, "Do you think we have more things in common with one another or more differences? Well, let's find out!"

Directions

Organize the chairs into a circle with one fewer chair than participants. As the facilitator, stand in the center of the circle and say, "I'm looking for someone, someone like me who _____" (this can either be an interest, like, or characteristic). Everyone who can relate to that statement must stand up out of his chair and go to another open seat. For example, "I'm looking for some-

---

Adapted from Williams, R. L., Lantz, A. E., and Noorulamin, S. (2008). *Making Smart Choices: Social Emotional Skills for Adolescent Girls*. Alexandria, VA: American School Counselor Association.

one, someone like me who likes Netflix." Everyone who likes Netflix must get up and move to a new open seat. We cannot return to our own chair or the chairs directly next to it on the left and right. The person remaining standing, without a chair, will now stand in the middle and begin the next round. If someone finds themselves in the middle multiple times, please ask them to select another group member who has not been in the middle as yet to come and take their place.

Repeat multiple times until all/most of the participants have had a chance to be in the middle. If the participants seem comfortable and ready to get more personal, have them change the game so they introduce something about their culture and/or family. Example: "I'm looking for someone, someone like me who speaks more than one language." These types of questions will allow the participants to connect on a deeper level while also challenging certain stereotypes and assumptions they may have made about each other.

Debrief

1. What was activity that like for you?

2. What did you find most enjoyable or challenging?

3. What was something new you learned about someone else?

4. How did you decide what to say when you were in the middle?

5. Why is it helpful to learn about each other?

6. If no one else moved when you asked your question, how did it feel?

7. How did this experience help break down stereotypes or assumptions?

8. What was the point of this exercise?

9. What did you learn from this experience?

10. How can we use what we learned in the future?

ACTIVITY: ESTABLISHING GUIDELINES

Objective

To create a common understanding of appropriate behavior so that all members feel physically and emotionally cared for.

Materials

One sheet of paper and a writing tool per group.

Introduction

Write the word *ROPES* on the board or on a large sheet of paper. Then ask the group, "How can ropes be used in real life?" Responses may include: can hold things together, help get you up a mountain, can tie someone up, keep you from falling, etc. "In our group, we will use the concept of ROPES to establish our boundaries while also maintaining enough flexibility so that we do not feel too constrained."

Directions

Divide participants into small teams and assign each group one or two letters of the word *ROPES*. Also give each team one sheet of paper and something to write with. Groups will then come up with rules/guidelines that begin with those letters that can help create a positive and safe environment for all. If time is limited, conduct the activity as a large group and go through each letter together, while writing responses on the board. Examples may include:

R:	Reach out for help, Respond kindly, Respect thoughts and feelings
O:	Offer support, Open minds, Own your part
P:	Patience, Participation, Provide ideas, Protect each other, Practice confidentiality
E:	Express honestly, Empathy, Energy, Educate
S:	Share, Show courage, Safety

Debrief

1. What did you enjoy about collaborating in a small group?

2. How did you communicate your ideas within the group?

3. How do we show others that we value their opinions?

4. Is there a difference between establishing our own guidelines versus having them dictated to us?

5. Which guideline is more important for you?

6. Which guideline will be most difficult for you to follow?

7. What does the term confidentiality mean and how does it relate to safety?

8. Who is responsible for making sure that these guidelines are being followed?

9. How will we respond if a guideline is not being followed?

10. What was the goal of this activity?

11. What is one rule you have established in your own life?

12. What is the purpose of having personal rules/guidelines in your own life?

ACTIVITY: ROCK-PAPER-SCISSORS TAG

Objective

To boost energy while also practicing collaboration, communication, and compromise.

Materials

None.

Introduction

Say to the group, "If rock, paper, and scissors were to play tag against other, I wonder who would win. What do you think? Well, let's find out!" Or, ask who among the group has played the Rock-Paper-Scissors game and then ask that individual to review the hierarchy of symbols for the others.

Directions

Creatively divide participants into two equal groups (i.e., Chocolate/Chips). A center line should be established where the two teams will eventually face off. Establish a safe zone 15 to 20 feet away from the center line behind each team. Allow 30 seconds for teams to huddle up and collectively decide on which "battle symbol" (rock, paper, or scissors) to throw upon returning to the

---

Adapted from MacIver, D. and McCarroll, L. (1997). *Initiatives, Games, & Activities: An Experiential Guide.* Aurora, CO: Adventures in Education.

center line to face off. When both teams are ready they will line up, parallel, on their side of the center line with one foot touching the line. Both teams will then shout, "Rock, paper, scissors, shoot!" All team members will flash the battle symbol that their team chose on the word *shoot*. The team that has the winning symbol must then try to tag/touch the members of the other team before they reach their safe zone. Anyone who is tagged then joins the other team, and the game continues indefinitely or until the two teams become one. Remind the group to participate respectfully and tag appropriately.

Even if all participants indicate that they are familiar with the rules, review the hierarchy of symbols to make sure everyone has the same understanding. This is especially helpful for those from different cultural backgrounds who may not have played before but are hesitant to ask for clarification: Rock smashes Scissors, Scissors cuts Paper, and Paper covers Rock.

Debrief

1. What was your favorite part of what we just did?

2. How did it feel to get tagged?

3. How did your team decide which symbol to throw?

4. What was the communication like on your team?

5. What kind of compromises did you make on your team?

6. What role did you play?

7. How was the attitude and energy on both teams?

8. What was the purpose of this?

9. How does it relate to collaboration and communication?

10. What is one thing you learned that you can use in your own life?

ACTIVITY: EARTH AROUND THE SUN

Objective

To practice attentive listening behaviors while engaging in face-to-face conversation.

Materials

One chair for every participant set up in two circles: one smaller inner circle and one lager outer circle, facing inward toward the smaller circle.

Introduction

Ask the group, "If the sun and the earth were to engage in conversation, who do you think would have better listening skills? I personally think the earth would struggle with making good eye contact because, remember, you're not supposed to look directly at the sun." Or, do a "round" and have each group member talk about how they know when someone is really listening to them: for example, good eye contact, head nodding, asking follow-up questions, or not multitasking.

Directions

Divide the large group into two even teams by counting off with "Earth" and "Sun." The facilitator can jump in if an additional person is needed. Each member of team Sun will take a seat in the inner circle facing out, and the Earths will sit in the outer circle, facing in toward the Suns. After briefly saying hello, shaking hands, and introducing themselves, the two partners will have one minute each to share their answers to the question being asked in that particular round (see questions below and adjust time as needed based on group size). Give a reminder to use attentive/good listening skills.

At the end of each round, partners will give each other a high five and say, "Thank you for sharing." The outer Earth circle will then rotate one spot to the right to face a new partner. After shaking hands and introducing themselves again, they will each respond to the question for that round. This rotation will continue until the Earth has gone completely around the Sun.

Sample Questions

1. What is the significance of your name (first and/or last)?

2. How do you respond to long lines?

3. What is one food that you can cook/prepare well?

4. Where do you like to sit in class?

5. What is your favorite quality about yourself?

6. How tall or short do you wish you were and why?

7. What is a quality that you appreciate in others?

8. When was the last time you called someone on the phone?

9. Netflix or movie theater?

10. What different types of water have you been in?

11. Apples or oranges?

12. Who is your favorite family member?

Debrief

1. What did we just do?

2. What is one word to describe your experience?

3. What did you like about being a Sun or an Earth?

4. How could you tell that your partner was really listening to you?

5. What communication skills were you intentionally trying to use?

6. Which question/round was your favorite?

7. How was this form of communication different from how you typically communicate?

8. Can you tell when someone is not really listening to you? How does that feel?

9. What was the purpose of this activity?

10. Based on this experience, what is one thing you will do differently from now on?

ACTIVITY: TENNIS BALL PASS

Objective

To practice patience, persistence, and creative ways to problem-solve as a team.

Materials

One to two tennis balls or other small, fairly soft balls.

Introduction

Ask the group, "What does it mean to *drop the ball*? How have you dropped the ball and fallen short of doing your part? Here is our chance to do our part for our team."

Directions

Have the group number off starting with one. Once numbered, give them 10 seconds to move anywhere they want in the room and then say, "Freeze!" Give the tennis ball to number one and instruct the group as follows:

The ball must pass from the hands of number one to the hands of number two and so on until everyone has received the ball. If the ball touches

---

Adapted from Williams, R. L., Lantz, A. E., and Noorulamin, S. (2008). *Making Smart Choices: Social and Emotional Skills for Adolescent Girls*. Alexandria, VA: American School Counselor Association.

the ground or if anybody talks at any point, the entire group must start over. The goal is to get the ball through everyone's hands, in numerical order, as fast as you can.

Ideally, the team will realize that they are able to move from their initial spot and stand in a circle format, close together, in numerical order, and pass the ball from one hand to the next. Allow them to struggle and reach this idea on their own. If they are really struggling and time is running out, ask them, "Did the rules say that you had to stay in the same spot you started in?"

If time allows and the group needs more of a challenge, do another round and add a second ball five seconds after the first ball has been started. The rules will remain the same with the second ball, and now both balls must make it through the entire group, as quickly as possible.

Debrief

1. Was the team successful the first time? How about the second?

2. Why didn't you give up after the first few failed attempts?

3. How did your team respond when a mistake was made?

4. How might attitude, negative or positive, impact the team?

5. What adjustments did you make along the way?

6. How does this relate to persistence?

7. What role did you play in this activity?

8. What is one thing you would do differently next time?

9. What was the purpose of this activity?

10. How does this connect back to your life?

ACTIVITY: MINEFIELD

Objective

To work as a team and practice communication while navigating through obstacles.

Materials

A variety of objects, equipment, or miscellaneous items such as stuffed animals, Koosh balls, Slinkys, small construction cones, paper, rope, water balloons, etc.

Introduction

Ask the group, "What do you think would help us get through a minefield if we could not see but we knew that danger was all around us?"

Directions

Using rope, caution tape, or chalk, create a large open "field" with a clear start and finish line. Spread out the various objects to represent land mines and place them on the ground or floor within the field.

Divide the large group into two teams, "Eyes" and "Ears." Give one team, Ears, a set of blindfolds and have them move to the starting line. Have team

---

Adapted from MacIver, D. and McCarroll, L. (1997). *Initiatives, Games, & Activities: An Experiential Guide.* Aurora, CO: Adventures in Education.

Eyes move to the finish line. Once blindfolds are in place, the fun begins, as the Eyes must get the Ears through the minefield without them stepping on a mine. Team Eyes cannot step into the field or touch anyone on the other team. Once every member of team Ears has made it safely through the minefield, the goal has been met! If time permits, allow teams to switch roles and go through the activity again so that team Eyes can experience the minefield as well.

Guard the safety of the group closely throughout this process and step in as needed at any point.

Debrief

1. Did you make it through the minefield successfully?

2. Who or what helped you along the way?

3. How did it feel as you were navigating your way across?

4. What is one thing you observed?

5. Did you trust your partner(s)? Why or why not?

6. What was it like when you made it to the other side?

7. What do the landmines represent?

8. Who or what helps you navigate around the landmines in your own life?

9. What was the purpose of this activity?

10. How does this activity relate to your own life?

ACTIVITY: SEPARATE THE "I" FROM THE "YOU"

Objective

To be clear, direct, and honest in expressing your thoughts and feelings, especially when addressing conflict.

Materials

Notecards/scraps of paper and writing utensils.

Introduction

As the facilitator, discuss a specific time when you were upset with a friend or family member, and instead of talking to the other person about it directly, you tried to ignore your feelings and just "get over it." Ask the group if they have ever done the same thing. The problem with the get-over-it strategy is that it usually builds resentment and regret over time because the actual issue and feelings remain unresolved. Then state, "I wish I could have just said what I needed to say, but I didn't know how to do it without blaming the other person. But now I do, and I'm going to tell you all about it."

Adapted from Williams, R. L., Lantz, A. E., and Noorulamin, S. (2008). *Making Smart Choices: Social and Emotional Skills for Adolescent Girls*. Alexandria, VA: American School Counselor Association.

Directions

Creatively divide the large group into teams of three and give them 47 seconds to create a team handshake. If time allows, have each team perform their handshake in front of the large group before beginning the activity. This is to build comfort and camaraderie.

Write the "I" Statement format (example below) on the board and ask participants to copy it down on their notecards as well. Emphasize that the point of this statement is to focus on the upsetting action/behavior rather than the person who engaged in it. After all, *someone* you like can do *something* you do not like. Also avoid using the word *you* as to minimize the other person becoming defensive and then not hearing what you are really trying to say.

"I" Statement Format:

I feel _____ (name the feeling)

When or because _____ (describe a specific behavior or action)

I would like _____ (describe exactly what you want)

Here is what you can count on from me _____ (describe your commitment to this process)

Next, allow one minute for each member of the small group (total of three minutes) to discuss a current problem they are having with a friend, family member, colleague, etc. This could include a friend being consistently late to pick you up, your colleague not doing her part of a collaborative project, or a stranger encroaching on your personal space. After each person has shared, the small group should then pick one of the scenarios to revisit and incorporate an "I" Statement in a role play. Time permitting, have each small group present their role play in front of the large group.

Examples:

1. I feel frustrated with being late, and I'd like for us to be more punctual.

2. I get overwhelmed when I have too much to do, and I'd like more balance in our collaboration.

3. I feel anxious when I don't have room to move around, so I'd like some more space.

Debrief

1. What was it like talking among your small group?

2. How do you typically address conflict?

3. Why do we hold back sometimes and not say what we really mean to say?

4. What could be the consequence of saying how you feel?

5. What could be the consequence of not saying how you feel?

6. How can using an "I" Statement benefit both you and the other person?

7. What did you learn about yourself through this activity?

8. What is the point of our conversation today?

9. How does this relate to healthy relationships and setting boundaries?

10. When will you use your "I" Statement next and with whom?

ACTIVITY: BLOB TAG

Objective

To have fun and get energized while discussing leadership and attitude.

Materials

None.

Introduction

Say to the group, "Have you ever heard that misery loves company? Well guess what, *positivity* loves company even more!"

Directions

Ask who among the group has a REALLY positive attitude today. The first person who raises his or her hand will then be "It" to start off this tag game. After clarifying the boundaries and reminding everyone to tag respectfully, the person who is It can then begin running around to tag and collect others to join his "blob." Each time someone is tagged, he or she then becomes "It" as well and links arms with the growing blob. The blob must stay connected the entire time until all participants have been tagged and, thus, become a part of the blob.

Adapted from MacIver, D. and McCarroll, L. (1997). *Initiatives, Games, & Activities: An Experiential Guide*. Aurora, CO: Adventures in Education.

Debrief

1. Share one word to describe your experience.

2. What did you find most enjoyable or challenging?

3. How did it feel to get tagged?

4. What did you notice as the blob got bigger?

5. How does this activity relate to attitude and energy?

6. What is the impact of positive leadership?

7. What allows someone to remain positive even through conflict or frustrations?

8. Why did we do this activity?

9. What is the significance for our group?

10. Based on this experience, what is one thing you will do differently in your own life?

ACTIVITY: TRUST WAVE

Objective

To practice taking risk and building trust among group members.

Materials

None.

Introduction

Share an example of when you have participated in a "human wave" during a sporting event, in a stadium, or maybe at a school assembly. Have the group then join you in creating a wave in which all group members will rise, one by one, while raising their arms in a fluid motion after the person before them has gone.

Directions

Creatively divide the large group into two smaller groups (i.e., Sun/Shine). Have each group form a straight line, shoulder to shoulder, facing toward the other group. To determine the distance between the two lines, have the participants extend their arms out in front of them at about shoulder height. Hands should approximately reach the wrists of the person across from them. This will be the **Wave** through which the **Runner** goes.

Adapted from MacIver, D. and McCarroll, L. (1997). *Initiatives, Games, & Activities: An Experiential Guide.* Aurora, CO: Adventures in Education.

The Runner will start from 10 feet away and then walk or run through the tunnel-like Wave. The participants in the lines will raise their arms right before the Runner reaches them and then will lower them as soon as soon as he passes by. It is important to have the Runner and the Wave communicate with each other before each attempt. For instance, the Runner would say his name and "Jack ready to run." The Wave would respond, "Run, Jack, run!" Jack then says, "Jack running" as he makes his way through the Wave tunnel.

All members of the Wave lines must be focused on the Runner at all times so they can judge his speed and raise their arms accordingly. Stop for safety checks throughout the activity and give positive feedback to the group for keeping each other safe. If time allows and all group members have gone, invite volunteers to go through again, especially if they were nervous or lacked trust during their first run.

Debrief

1. Share one word to describe how you felt during this activity.

2. What allowed you to push past your hesitations and go through the Wave?

3. What was your role throughout this process?

4. How did you know the "Wave" was trustworthy?

5. Did anyone get hurt? What would we have done if someone did get hurt?

6. What was key to the success of this activity?

7. What was the point of doing this?

8. How does this activity relate to relationships?

9. What is one thing you learned that you will apply to your own life?

ACTIVITY: I GOT YOUR BACK—TRUST LEAN

Objective

To practice being trusting and trustworthy while communicating personal needs.

Materials

None.

Introduction

Talk about someone in your life who you can rely on and share an example of how he or she has supported you during a difficult time. Then ask the group, "Who is someone in your life who has always got your back?"

Directions

Instruct the group to line up according to height in 27 seconds. This allows them to be nearer to an appropriately sized partner for this activity. Now have them select a partner of similar size or strength. Have the pair quickly come up with a team name to build comfort and begin communication.

Each team will designate a SPOTTER and FALLER. The faller should stand upright with their body rigid and their arms across their chest. The

---

Adapted from MacIver, D. and McCarroll, L. (1997). *Initiatives, Games, & Activities: An Experiential Guide.* Aurora, CO: Adventures in Education.

spotter should stand about a foot behind the faller in the spotting position (feet straddled for stability with both hands up to protect the head and shoulders). The spotter should then place their hands on the back of the faller and exchange the following verbal commands:

FALLER: "Ready to fall"--------SPOTTER: "Ready to spot"

FALLER: "Falling"----------------SPOTTER: "Fall on"

At this point, the faller leans backward, remaining rigid at the waist with heels remaining on the floor. The spotter allows the faller to lean back about a foot and then gently pushes them back to the starting position. If this feels comfortable, the faller may choose to step forward about six inches and repeat the process. The distance between the faller and spotter should not exceed three feet. Allow partners to switch roles so that both may experience being the faller and the spotter.

Debrief

1. What was the fall like?

2. How did your level of comfort and trust change throughout the process?

3. How did your team establish communication?

4. What were you most nervous about?

5. How did you decide how far to fall?

6. What did your partner do that was helpful?

7. How does this relate to trust in relationships?

8. How can trust get damaged?

9. What can be done to restore trust?

10. What is one thing that surprised you?

ACTIVITY: HUMAN SPRING

Objective

To explore balance, communication, and boundaries in relationships.

Materials

None.

Introduction

Tell the group about a time when you felt off balance and you needed someone else's help to get your feet back on the ground, literally or figuratively. Examples might include feeling overwhelmed with work, having too many responsibilities at home, or putting more effort into a relationship than you were receiving in return. Also talk about who or what helped you become stable once again.

Directions

Allow 51 seconds for the group to line up according to the size of their hands. This will begin communication and build comfort with touch. Have participants partner up with someone who has a similar hand size.

Adapted from MacIver, D. and McCarroll, L. (1997). *Initiatives, Games, & Activities: An Experiential Guide*. Aurora, CO: Adventures in Education.

Have the partners face one another approximately 18 inches apart with their arms out in front of them, palms facing their partner, at shoulder height. They will now count to three and fall toward each other, where their hands will meet in the middle. They should catch each other with their palms and gently push each other back up to the starting position. This process is repeated until both partners feel comfortable and confident in their ability to catch the other. When ready, both partners should step back six inches and repeat the exercise. This can be continued until the distance is deemed too far to safely stop each other from falling.

Although it is ideal to have partners of similar height and weight, this activity can be done successfully even among people of varying sizes, as long as there is clear communication.

Debrief

1. What was this experience like for you?

2. How did you feel when your hands met your partner's in the middle?

3. What happened when your partner wanted to take a bigger risk than you did?

4. How did you communicate your needs?

5. In what ways did you show respect?

6. How does this activity relate to relationships, including friendships?

7. How can a relationship become off balance?

8. Why do you think we did this activity?

9. What did you learn about yourself?

ACTIVITY: THE PERSON I SEE

Objective

To examine our self-talk, become more self-aware, and practice being better friends to ourselves.

Materials

A small mirror taped in a box with a lid.

Introduction

How you introduce this activity is very important. Hold the box in your hands and explain, "When you open the box you will see somebody that you recognize. And even though we all know the person in the box, it is still important to keep it a secret until everyone has had chance to peek."

Directions

Pass the box around and have each participant give a nonphysical compliment to the person they see inside. Ask them to open the box and say, "The person I see is _____." For example, "This person I see is smart." After the compliment, nothing more is to be said as the box is then gently handed to the next person in the circle.

Adapted from Williams, R. L., Riedo, S., and DeBard, S. (2007). *A Handbook for Leading Positive Youth Development Programs*. Denver, CO: Smart-Girl, Inc.

Have the group pass the box around again, and this time they must give a physical compliment to the person they see in the box. For example, "The person I see has great skin." Continue on and, if time allows, do a third round in which participants can choose to give either a physical or internal compliment to the person in the box. Pass the box and have them look inside throughout every round.

Debrief

1. What did we just do?

2. How many compliments do you give to others on any given day?

3. What was fun or challenging about giving yourself a compliment?

4. What is one fear you had as the box approached you?

5. Describe the difference between being confident and conceited.

6. What is self-talk and how does it impact you?

7. How do you feel when you are in the company of someone who is confident?

8. How can someone else's positive or negative self-concept impact you?

9. What is the purpose of this activity?

10. What is the benefit of positive self-talk?

11. If you had a friend who talked to you the way that you talk to yourself, how much time would you want to spend with that person? Why?

12. What is one thing you will do from now on to be a better friend to yourself?

ACTIVITY: THE CYCLE OF INFLUENCE

Objective

To identify the various factors that influence our self-talk and self-concept. Recognize the positive messages and learn how to filter out the negative ones.

Materials

White board or large paper, markers.

Introduction

In a round, have the group answer, "Who do you think has a more positive self-concept: Mickey Mouse or Minnie Mouse, and why?" Also have the group clarify what *self-concept* means (i.e., a collection of thoughts, values, and beliefs about oneself).

Directions

On the board, draw an image similar to the one below with the four categories: **Media, Other People, Self-Talk, and Self-Concept.** The square around Self-Concept represents the Confidence Shield, which serves as our filter for unconstructive messages.

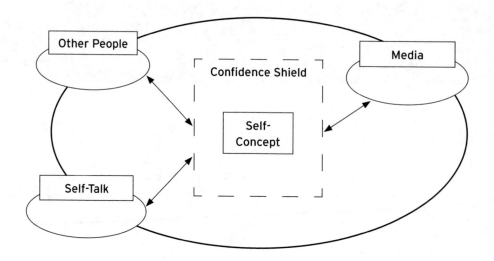

Instruct group members to find two partners who have on the most similar-looking clothing as them (such as shirt or sock color or type of shoe). In their triads, have them complete the phrase, "My self-concept is influenced by _____." Examples include: comments from others, magazine ads, family, culture, etc. Allow three minutes for this conversation so that all group members can share.

Next, have each team rotate through and write in their stated influences in the corresponding categories on the board. Under the Media category, for instance, one might write in YouTube, Instagram, or magazines. If their comment has already been listed, they can circle the item on the board instead. For example, if someone has already written "friends" as an influence in the Other People category, or "putting myself down" in the Self-Talk circle, the next person can simply circle those comments upon reaching the board for their turn. Continue until all teams have recorded their answers on the board.

Debrief

1. Share one word to describe your reaction to this exercise.

2. What do you see depicted on the board?

3. What types of messages do you receive from any of the categories on the board about yourself?

4. How can you filter and limit the negative messages in your life?

5. What weakens or strengthens your Confidence Shield?

6. How do all of these categories impact each other?

7. What is the purpose of this activity?

8. How does this conversation relate to you as a person?

9. What impacted you most?

10. What will you do now with the information we have learned?

ACTIVITY: CHALLENGING STEREOTYPES

Objective

To examine what stereotypes are and explore the consequences of perpetuating assumptions and uninformed judgments.

Materials

Sticky notes, markers/pens.

Introduction

Share an anecdote of when you stereotyped someone but then were proven wrong upon gaining more information about them. Ask a member of the group to share an additional example from their own experience.

Directions

Engage the group in a conversation about stereotypes by asking the following questions:

1. What is a stereotype?

2. Who has ever assumed something about someone else, based on the way they look or based on their group association?

3. What are the various types of social groups/cliques that get stereotyped?

As the participants are listing off the different groups, write the groups on the board and try to consolidate them into four to five groups total (i.e., popular, nerds, smokers, band geeks). Realizing that not everyone may agree on the mentioned categories, allow time for discussion so all voices can be heard.

Give each participant four to five sticky notes and instruct them to write down one stereotype they have made or that they have heard others make about each particular group listed on the board. For example, a common stereotype for the Popular group could be that they are rich or stuck-up. You would write down "rich" on one sticky note and then place it on the board in the corresponding column. Allow participants three to five minutes to write down the stereotypes and put them on the board. Encourage the group to remain silent until all participants have placed their sticky notes on the board.

After all of the students have placed their sticky notes in the respective categories, ask them to take a look at the board and point to the group with whom they identify most closely. If they don't feel like they belong in any of the groups, ask them what group others might assume they are a part of. If they are still unsure of others' opinion of them, ask them to think about a friend or family member and to which group they might belong.

Ask for volunteers to collect the sticky notes from each column. Make sure to keep the notes separated by the categories they were placed in on the board. While the rest of the group remains silent, have each volunteer read every sticky note, one by one, with absolutely no commentary or responses from the crowd.

Note: Depending on the level of safety, maturity, and trust among the group, this activity can be done to include categories of race or religion instead of social groups.

Debrief

1. What was that like for volunteers who read the sticky notes?

2. How did it feel, for others, to sit back and just listen to comments being read?

3. How many of us have ever stereotyped someone else in real life?

4. How many of you have ever felt judged based on your physical appearance or the group you hang out with?

5. How does it feel to be judged or stereotyped?

6. How can stereotyping be harmful to you and to others?

7. Who perpetuates or continues the cycle of stereotyping?

8. Can this cycle be stopped? If so, who can change it?

9. How can it benefit you to reach out and get to know people outside of your social group?

10. What makes us hesitant to get to know new people who may appear different from us?

11. What is one thing that you can do to limit the amount of judgments you make about others?

12. Why did we do this activity?

13. Based on this experience, what is one thing you will do differently in your own life?

ACTIVITY: I AM _____, BUT I AM NOT _____

Objective

To understand how stereotypes can be inaccurate or incomplete.

Materials

Notecards or sticky name tags/labels, paper, something to write with.

Introduction

Ask the group to define the word *stereotype* and give a few examples of stereotypes in the school or work setting.

Directions

Instruct the group to make a list of the different ways they identify or their group associations. For example: an athlete, thespian, White, Hispanic, American, man, woman, teenager, etc. Now have them circle the identity that is most important to them and then list a stereotype that is associated with that identity. This may be a stereotype that they have heard, seen, or one that has been made about them personally.

Now have them write the statement, "I am _____, but I am not _____." In the first part of the statement they will write in who they identify as. In the second part they will challenge a stereotype that has been made about them based on that identity. For example, "I am female, but I do not cook" or "I am Black, but I am not an athlete." Allow two to three minutes for participants to write down their statements.

Have the participants turn to the person sitting next to them and share their statement. Bring the group back together after two minutes and invite volunteers to share their statement out loud. Instruct them not to say anything before or immediately after to validate their statement. Then, go around the circle and ask each participant to share what he or she wrote so that all may practice taking a risk and being heard. Make sure to remind the group not to comment or question others' statement during the activity.

If time remains after everyone has shared, allow participants to do another round and make an additional statement. After everyone has had a turn, pause and take a deep breath as a group, as this process can be quite intense and uncomfortable for many.

Debrief

1. What emotions came up for you during this activity?

2. How does it feel to be stereotyped?

3. Why do we stereotype others or even ourselves sometimes?

4. Why is assuming easier than asking?

5. What do we risk by making judgments about others?

6. How are stereotypes incomplete?

7. Why do we sometimes go along with a stereotype that is made about us, even if that's not who we really are?

8. What do you think was the main purpose of this activity?

9. What is one thing you learned about someone else in this group today?

10. What did you learn about yourself?

11. What is one thing you will do differently from now on?

ACTIVITY: IMPACTED BY BULLYING NOTECARDS

Objective

To reflect on past experiences, demonstrate empathy, and encourage positive future behavior.

Materials

Notecards and pens/pencils.

Introduction

Share a personal story of when you were impacted by bullying. This could be about you or even someone you care about.

Directions

First, mix up the circle and have the group get in order by their birthday. Once seated, have participants shake hands with both people next to them (left and right) and say their name with a funny accent. This is to build comfort and connection before diving into a high-risk conversation.

Next, on their notecards have everyone respond to the statement, "I've been impacted by bullying when…" For example, "I've been impacted by bullying when my little sister felt afraid to go to school because of a rumor that had been spread about her." Or, "I was impacted by bullying in the seventh grade when I was the bully and took my jokes too far about my friend's weight. He eventually stopped hanging out with me." This is a silent, anonymous activity, so **<u>no names</u>** should be written on the notecards.

After one to two minutes, collect all of the notecards, shuffle, and redistribute among the group to be read aloud.

Debrief

1. What did we just do?

2. How did it feel to write down your story and have it shared?

3. What was that like for you to hear about others' experiences?

4. Based on what you've heard today, what are different bullying behaviors?

5. How does bullying impact us and others?

6. Who can engage in bullying behaviors?

7. How do we make others feel unvalued, sometimes unintentionally?

8. How can you tell if it is bullying or just joking around, and why is it important to know the difference?

9. What is the purpose of this activity?

10. What is one change you are going to make?

ACTIVITY: A.C.T.I.O.N. (ANTI-BULLYING)

Objective

To identify bullying behaviors, understand the difference between a bystander and an UPstander, and create a support system in which people empathize with and care for one another.

Materials

Have sample scenarios available (see below).

Introduction

Survey the group and ask, "Who has ever stood up for someone else? Why did you do it? How did it feel? Being a support for others is not only important; it also feels good to do the right thing. However, it can be nerve-wracking and scary at times. So, we are going to learn six different ways to take ACTION and intervene so that we are prepared in the future."

Directions

Have the group define and describe the difference between a "bystander" and an "UPstander." Make sure they understand that a bystander observes,

Adapted from Williams, R. L., Lantz, A. E., and Noorulamin, S. (2008). *Making Smart Choices: Social and Emotional Skills for Adolescent Girls.* Alexandria, VA: American School Counselor Association.

while an UPstander takes action to help others. Discuss and demonstrate each of the A.C.T.I.O.N. steps below or have volunteers briefly model each step. Ask the group to evaluate if it is a "high-risk" or "low-risk" intervention for the UPstander. The answers will vary depending on our individual personalities and comfort levels.

After introducing each of the A.C.T.I.O.N. steps, divide the participants into groups of three or four. Ask them to create a scenario/role play in which bullying is taking place at school, in the workplace, or even in their families. Each participant will play a role (target, bully, bystander, UPstander) in the scene. The UPstander in each scenario will demonstrate how to intervene using one or two of the A.C.T.I.O.N. strategies. Allow two to four minutes for groups to develop their skits or talk through their scenario. Make sure to circulate among the groups to guide them in the appropriate direction. Once they are all ready, have each group present its skit or share the scenario to the large group.

If a group is struggling with coming up with an idea, present the options below:

1. One of your friends gossiping about what another friend posted on social media.

2. You are in the cafeteria during lunch when two of your friends start talking about another student's clothing.

3. You are hanging out with your family when one of your older family members says, "That's retarded" in reference to something they didn't like.

4. Your co-workers are talking poorly about another colleague.

5. You are in class and observe someone say, "That's so gay" in response to a surprise quiz that was just announced.

A.C.T.I.O.N Steps:

A—Assert Yourself

Speak up! Interrupt the situation. Say, "I'm not okay with what you're doing. Stop it."

C—Create a Distraction

Talk to the bully about something else.
Take the attention off of the target and the situation.

T—Turn to Others

There is strength in numbers. Get help from others.
Confront the bully in a group rather than alone.

I—Include

Take the person who is being bullied away from the situation and *include* him/her into your group or activity.

O—Offer Support

Tell the person being bullied you are sorry it happened and ask him/her if there is anything you can do. Offer comfort.

N—Notify an Adult

Tell an adult about what is taking place or what you suspect is about to take place.
Sometimes there is only so much you can do by yourself.
Follow through and keep trying until an adult does something to help.

Debrief

1. What did this activity help you realize?

2. Have you ever helped someone who was being bullied? How did that feel?

3. How does it feel to have someone intervene on your behalf?

4. How can you teach others to be UPstanders?

5. What will happen if there are more UPstanders and fewer bystanders?

6. How does silence perpetuate bullying?

7. How has your perception of bullying changed?

8. How might the world be a different place if there were more UPstanders?

9. What makes it difficult to be an UPstander?

10. Which A.C.T.I.O.N. step are you most and least comfortable with?

11. What is the point of this conversation?

12. How does this apply to you?

13. Who is one person you would like to apologize to for being unkind to, or one person you would like to thank for being an UPstander?

ACTIVITY: FLIRTING VS. HURTING (SEXUAL HARASSMENT PREVENTION)

Objective

To define and discuss the impact of sexual harassment versus flirting. To also explore reciprocity, consent, asserting yourself, and intervening on behalf of others.

Materials

Whiteboard or large paper.

Introduction

Do a round in which everyone shares or models one strategy that they use to get the attention of someone they like (i.e., winking, sitting next to in class, giving a gift, telling jokes). Then ask them, "How do you know if someone is giving you the green light, the yellow light, or a red light in response?"

Directions

Prior to beginning the activity, take five minutes to discuss the definition of sexual harassment and its various components. The definition for sexual

---

Adapted from Williams, R. L., Lantz, A. E., and Noorulamin, S. (2008). *Making Smart Choices: Social and Emotional Skills for Adolescent Girls*. Alexandria, VA: American School Counselor Association.

Activity from Strauss, S. (1992). *Sexual Harassment and Teens: A Program for Positive Change*. Minneapolis, MN: Free Spirit Publishing.

harassment is ***"any unwanted request for sexual favors, or verbal or physical conduct of a sexual nature."***

Have group members give an example of:

1. "Verbal conduct of a sexual nature."

2. Examples: sexual rumors, jokes, graffiti, sexually explicit language, calling someone a hunk/babe, whistling/catcalls, discussing others' sexual identity, rating someone's physical appearance, name-calling.

3. "Physical conduct of a sexual nature."

4. Examples: touching someone in a sexual manner, swatting, hugging, kissing, snapping a bra, depantsing, rubbing oneself sexually around others, talking about someone's body parts, suggestive body language.

5. "Request for sexual favors."

6. Examples: asking that someone perform a sexual act in return for something else, suggesting that someone "owes" you sex for taking them on a date or to a dance.

Next, draw the diagram below on the board and begin the next activity:

Flirting		Hurting/Sexual Harassment (Unwelcomed, not mutual)	
Behavior	Feelings	Behavior	Feelings
Eye Contact	Exciting		

Begin with the Flirting side of the chart and remind the group that flirting implies that it is mutual and wanted (i.e., you like them and they like you; both people are giving the "green light" of consent). Ask group members what they might identify as flirting behaviors. Give the first example of "eye contact" yourself and demonstrate how eye contact might be flirting. Ask how it would feel if you shared eye contact with someone you liked. Have the group give five to six examples of behaviors that other people do when they flirt, as well as the feelings that might come as a result of that behaviors (i.e., eye contact may feel exciting, touch could feel loving).

Next, move on to the other side of the chart and ask about sexual harassment behaviors. Remember, if it's sexual harassment, then it is unwanted and not mutual. As the group facilitator, you will again go first and use the same example of *eye contact*. Demonstrate or ask how eye contact might be a sexually harassing behavior (looking at someone's body parts instead of looking at their face). Ask the group members how that might feel. Have them continue and identify other sexually harassing behaviors, and be sure to list how that would make them feel if it happened to them. Many of the sexually harassing behaviors may be the same as the flirting behaviors, but the feelings will be different.

If time allows or as an additional activity on another day, have the group practice "I" Statements to assert their boundaries and feelings, as well as apply A.C.T.I.O.N steps to speak up for others.

Debrief

1. What do you notice about the chart we have drawn?

2. What are the similarities and differences between the two sides?

3. How can knowing the difference between flirting and hurting protect you as well as others?

4. Who can engage in sexual harassment or flirting (boy-boy, boy-girl, girl-boy, girl-girl)?

5. Where does sexual harassment take place? How about flirting?

6. How can name-calling or rumors be sexual harassment?

7. Describe how it might feel to be sexually harassed.

8. How can you tell that someone else might be feeling uncomfortable or harassed?

9. How can someone use an "I" Statement to express their boundaries?

10. What are the similarities between sexual harassment and bullying?

11. How can you be an UPstander and help someone who is being sexually harassed?

12. How can you use the "traffic light" to help you gauge if someone is interested in you?

13. What do you do if you get a "red light"?

14. Why is it important for us to understand what sexual harassment is?

15. What is one thing that you will do differently from now on?

ACTIVITY: KEEP YOURSELF IN CHECK

Objective

To examine and adjust one's own attitude and behaviors that may be socially aggressive, unproductive, or unhealthy in relationships.

Materials

A copy of the Social Aggression Checklist for every person, and pens or pencils.

Introduction

Ask the group, "How do you usually communicate that you are upset with someone?"

Directions

Give everyone a copy of the Social Aggression Checklist and something to write with. Give them 10 seconds to find a spot in the room that is comfortable and not too close to anyone else. Allow five minutes to complete the Checklist and then return to the circle for further discussion.

Social Aggression Checklist

Circle all statements that describe a behavior that you have engaged in:

1. When I am angry with someone, that person is often the last to know it.

2. When I am frustrated with my partner/colleague/friend, I give that person the silent treatment.

3. When I do not like someone's personality, I derive a certain degree of pleasure when a friend listens to me talk about this person and agrees with my assessment of the person.

4. I contribute to the rumor mill in my family and/or at work.

5. I break a friend's confidentiality to have a good story to tell to someone else.

6. I confront people in public who are close to me—particularly when they don't think, feel, or behave like I do.

7. I often criticize people who are close to me—particularly when they don't think, feel, or behave like I do.

8. I intentionally exclude friends from activities to make a point with them.

9. I have attempted to "steal" a rival's friend or partner.

10. When I am angry with a friend, I have threatened to sever the relationship in hopes that the person will comply with my wishes.

11. I want others to feel angry toward a person when I am angry with that person.

12. It is easy for me to believe negative things about other people.

13. I talk about others because they talk about me.

14. It is difficult for me to hear about good things that happen to people I do not like.

15. I am jealous of other people (e.g., what they have, how they look, or talents they possess).

16. Once someone "wrongs me," I cannot forgive them easily and I must get them back.

17. If a colleague or family member is getting too much attention, I may initiate a rumor or negative information about that person to keep her/him in her/his "place."

18. I regularly compete with other people, and sometimes I don't even realize I am doing it.

Adapted from Field, J. E., Kolbert, J. B., Crothers, L. M., & Hughes, T. (2009). *Understanding Girl Bullying and What to Do About It: Strategies to Help Heal the Divide.* Thousand Oaks, CA: Corwin Press.

DEBRIEF

1. How many statements did you circle?

2. How did you feel as you read through each item?

3. Any new insights?

4. Was there anything specifically that made you feel proud or disappointed?

5. What does it mean to be "socially aggressive"?

6. How can engaging in aggressive behaviors impact a relationship?

7. How does this checklist relate to bullying?

8. What was the point of us doing this activity?

9. How did your perspective change?

10. Based on what you learned about yourself, what is one change you are going to make?

ACTIVITY: COMPLIMENT COLLECTION

Objective

To show thanks and celebrate the others in the group.

Materials

Paper lunch bags, markers, paper, any additional art supplies that are available.

Introduction

Ask the group, "Have you ever wanted to say something nice to someone else, but you didn't really know how to go about it?" Sometimes it can feel uncomfortable or vulnerable to say something positive or recognize that you admire someone else in the group. As the group comes to a close, this is a great time to say thank you, give a compliment, or say something positive to each other in honor of the time we have spent together.

Directions

Give everyone a paper sack and art supplies so they can personalize/decorate their own Compliment Bags. Allow 20 to 30 minutes for them to design their bags as well as write a compliment to put in every group member's bag as well. It may be helpful to have all group member's names written on the board as to ensure proper spelling and to make sure that everyone is included. Ask the group to be genuine and sincere throughout this activity.

After everyone has completed their bags and finished distributing their compliments, bring them back together in a circle so they can read through their compliments. Have them select their favorite one to share aloud in a "round."

Debrief

1. How did it feel to give others compliments?

2. What was it like receiving compliments?

3. What was meaningful about this exercise?

4. How can you remember to give yourself compliments in the future?

5. Why is it important to celebrate others?

6. What did you observe?

7. What was the point of doing this?

8. How do you typically respond when someone gives you a compliment?

9. What did you learn about yourself?

10. How does this help us say "goodbye" to one another as the group comes to a close?

ACTIVITY: STRING GAME

Objective

To reflect on our experience together and bring closure to the group.

Materials

Yarn and scissors.

Introduction

Do a round in which everyone shares one way of saying goodbye (e.g., "Hasta luego," "Later gator," "Adios," "Ciao," "Arrivederci," "See you on the flip side"). Or ask, "How do you typically say goodbye in your family?"

Directions

Have the group sit or stand in a circle and hand one person the yarn to begin. Upon receiving yarn, each person will wrap the thread around their wrist, about three times around like a bracelet. As they wrap, each group member then shares one thing they learned from this group or one thing they will remember most. They will then toss the yarn to another group member and say something positive about that person. Keep going around until everyone has spoken. Then cut the string so that everyone may take a portion of the yarn with them. This represents their link to the group and their shared experience.

Debrief

1. What did we just do?

2. What does this web represent?

3. Why is it important to reflect on our experiences together?

4. How will we remain connected even after we say goodbye?

5. How will you continue this work outside of our group?

References

Adler, M. (1995). Homogeneity or heterogeneity of groups: When, and along what dimensions? *Canadian Journal of Counselling*, 29, 14–29.

American School Counselor Association, (2016). *ASCA Ethical standards for school counselors*. Retrieved from http://tinyurl.com/gszcbhy.

Antze, P. (1979). Role of ideologies in peer psychotherapy groups. In M. Lieberman & M. Lieberman (Eds.), *Self-Help Groups for Coping with Crises* (272–304). San Francisco, CA: Jossey-Bass Press.

Association for Specialists in Group Work. (2000). *Professional standards for the training of group workers*. Retrieved from http://tinyurl.com/y454dkdm.

Bailey D. F. & Bradbury-Bailey M. E. (2007). Promoting achievement for African-American males through group work. *Journal for Specialists in Group Work*, 32(1), 83–96.

Bell, K. & Norwood K. (2007). Gender equity intersects with mathematics and technology: Problem-solving education for changing times. In D. S. Sadker (Ed.), *Gender in the Classroom: Foundations, Skills, Methods, and Strategies Across the Curriculum* (225–258). Mahwah, NJ: Lawrence Erlbaum Associates.

Bemak, F., Chung, R. C.-Y., & Siroskey-Sabdo, L. (2005). Empowerment groups for academic success: An innovative approach to prevent high school failure for at-risk, urban African-American girls. *Professional School Counselor*, 8, 377–389.

119

Brown, N. (2009). *Becoming a group leader.* Upper Saddle River, NJ: Pearson Education.

Bryan, J., Steen, S. & Day-Vines, N. L. (2016). Psychoeducational groups in schools. In B. Erford, *Group Work in Schools* (2nd ed.), (207–224). New York, NY: Routledge.

Campbell. C. A. & Myrick, R. D. (1990). Motivational group counseling for low-performing students. *Journal for Specialists in Group Work*, 15(1), 43–50.

Conley, D. (2007). *Toward a more comprehensive conception of college readiness.* Eugene, OR: Educational Policy Improvement.

Corey, G., Corey, M. S., Callahan, P., & Russell, J. M. (2004). *Group Techniques.* Pacific Grove, CA: Brooks/Cole.

DeRosier, M. E. (2004). Building relationships and combating bullying: Effectiveness of a school-based social skills group intervention. *Journal of Clinical Child and Adolescent Psychology*, 33(1), 196–201.

Duckworth, A. P., Peterson, C., Matthews, M. D., & Kelly, D. R. (2007). Grit: perseverance and passion for long-term goals. *Journal of Personality and Social Psychology*, 92(6), 1087–1101.

Dweck, C. S., Walton, G. M., & Cohen, G. L. (2011). *Academic tenacity: Mindsets and skills that promote long-term learning.* Seattle, WA: Gates Foundation.

Erford, B. (2011). The ASCA National Model: Developing a comprehensive, developmental school counseling program. In B. Erford, *Transforming the school counseling profession* (44–57). Upper Saddle River, NJ: Pearson.

Farkas, G. (2003). Cognitive skills and noncognitive traits and behaviors in stratification processes. *Annual Review of Sociology*, 29, 541–562.

Farrington, C. R. (2012). *Teaching to adolescents to become learners. The role of noncognitive factors in shaping school performance: A critical literature review.* Chicago, IL: University of Chicago Consortium on Chicago School Research.

Field, J., Kolbert, J. B., Crothers, L. M., & Hughes, T. E. (2009). *Understanding Girl Bullying and What to Do About It: Strategies to Help Heal the Divide.* Thousand Oaks, CA: Corwin Press.

Gladding, S. T. (2008*). Groups: A counseling specialty, 6th ed.* Princeton, NJ: Merrill.

Glaser, J. (2004). *Leading through collaboration: Guiding groups to productive solutions.* New York, NY: Corwin Press.

Hess, D. (2007). Heterogeneous and homogeneous groups in the innovation process. *Oldenburger Studien zur Europäisierung und zur transnationalen Regulierung.* Oldenburg, Germany (ISSN: 1866-8798).

Kolbert, J., Williams, R. L., Morgan, L. M., Crothers, L. M., & Hughes, T. L. (2016). *Introduction to professional school counseling: Advocacy, leadership, and intervention.* New York, NY: Routledge.

LeCroy, C. W. & Daley, J. (2001). *Empowering adolescent girls: Examining the present and building skill for the future with the Go Grrrls Program.* New York, NY: W.W. Norton.

Lieberman, M. (1990, Oct). Understanding how groups work: A study of homogeneous peer group failures. *International Journal of Group Psychotherapy,* 40(1), 31–52.

MacIver, D. M. & McCarroll, L. (1997). *Initiatives, games & activities: An experiential guide.* Aurora, CO: Adventures in Education.

Malekoff, A. (2004). *Group work with adolescents: Principles and practice.* New York, NY: Guilford Press.

May, M. H. & Housley, W. (1996). The effects of group counseling on the self-esteem of sexually abused female adolescents. *Guidance & Counseling,* 11(4), 38–42.

Paisley, P. M. & Milsom, A. (2007). Group work as an essential contribution to transforming school counseling. *Journal for Specialists in Group Work,* 32(1), 9–17.

Perusse, R. G., Goodnough, G. E., & Lee, V. V. (2009). Group counseling in the school. *Psychology in the Schools,* 46, 225–231.

Powell, W. (1990). Neither market nor hierarchy: Network forms of organization. *Research in Organizational Behavior,* 12, 295–336.

Rapin, L. & Keel, L. (1998, revised 2007). *ASGW Best Practice Guidelines.* Retrieved from http://tinyurl.com/y5efuhwx

Rosen, K. H. & Bezold, A. (1996). Dating violence prevention: A didactic support group for young women. *Journal of Counseling and Development*, 74(5), 512–525.

Sax, L. (2005). *Why gender matters: What parents and teachers need to know about the emerging science of sex difference.* New York, NY: Doubleday.

Shechtman, Z., Bar-El O., & Hadar, E. (1997). Therapeutic factors and psychoeducational groups for adolescents: A comparison. *Journal for Specialists in Group Work*, 22(3), 203–213. From doi.org/10.1080/01933929708414381.

Southern, J. A., Erford, B. T., Vernon, A., & Davis-Gage, D. (2010). The value of group work: Functional group models and historical perspectives. In B. Erford (Ed.), *Group work in the schools.* Boston, MA: Pearson Education.

Steen, S. & Kaffenberger, C. (2007). Integrating academic interventions into small-group counseling in elementary school. *Professional School Counselor*, 10, 516–519.

Stone, C. (2013). *School counseling principles: Ethics and law* (3rd ed). Alexandria, VA: American School Counselor Association.

Strauss, S. (1992). *Sexual Harassment and Teens: A Program for Positive Change.* Minneapolis, MN: Free Spirit Publishing.

Thomas, R. & Pender, D. A. (2008). Association for specialists in group work: Best practice guidelines, 2007 revisions. *Journal for Specialists in Group Work*, 33(2), 111–117. From doi.org/10.1080/01933920801971184.

Tuckman, B. & Jensen, M. C. (1977). Stages of small-group development revisited. *Group and Organizational Studies, 2,* 419–427. From doi.org/10.1080/01933920801971184.

Veach, L. G. & Gladding, S. T. (2007). Using creative group techniques in high schools. *Journal for Specialists in Group Work*, 32(1), 71–81.

Williams, R. L. & Ferber, A. (2008). Facilitating Smart-Girl: Feminist pedagogy in service learning in action. *Feminist Teacher*, 19(1), 47–67.

Williams, R. L., Lantz, A. E., & Noorulamin, S. (2008). *Making smart choices: Social and emotional skills for adolescent girls.* Alexandria, VA: American School Counselor Association.

Williams, R. L., Riedo, S., & DeBard, S. (2007). *A handbook for leading positive youth development programs*. Denver, CO: Smart-Girl, Inc.

Wilson, F. R. (2010). Planning for group work in schools. In B. T. Erford (Ed.), *Group Work in the Schools* (1st ed.). Boston, MA: Pearson Education.

Yalom, I. D. (1985). *The Theory and Practice of Group Psychotherapy*, (3rd ed). New York, NY: Basic Books.

About the Authors

Rhonda Williams, EdD: Dr. Williams spent 25 years as a public educator and a school counselor before the natural transition as a counselor educator. She is a professor in the Counseling and Human Services Department at the University of Colorado, Colorado Springs, where she serves as the School Counseling Program Coordinator. Dr. Williams is committed to instilling in students the American School Counselor Association (ASCA) National Model and the *Ethical Standards for School Counselors*. Dr. Williams has served as President of the both Colorado and Kansas School Counselor Associations. She has been honored as the Colorado Middle School Counselor of the Year, the ASCA Middle School Counselor of the Year, and the ASCA Counselor Educator of the Year. She was recently awarded the inaugural Rhonda Williams Lifetime Achievement Award from the Colorado School Counselor Association (CSCA). Dr. Williams was the co-coordinator for the White House's and the First Lady's Reach Higher Convening at the University of Colorado, Colorado Springs in the summer of 2016. One of the most exciting parts of her profession is training groups of educators on team building, group facilitation, and advisory programs.

Sameen Noorulamin DeBard, MEd: Ms. DeBard currently serves a high school counselor. She has been involved with leading groups, as well as teaching the facilitation process, for the past fifteen years. Ms. DeBard spent twelve years working as a group facilitator, trainer, and director of programs for Smart-Girl, Inc. She has provided training for teachers and school counselors throughout the United States on effective facilitation skills for small groups and advisory programs. Ms. DeBard is an adjunct faculty member at the University of Colorado, Colorado Springs and a group facilitation trainer/consultant. She received her undergraduate degree in business administration and management from the University of Colorado, Boulder and her master's degree in counseling and human services from the University of Colorado, Colorado Springs.

Joseph Wehrman, PhD: Dr. Wehrman is an associate professor and department chair in the Department of Counseling and Human Services at the University of Colorado, Colorado Springs (UCCS). He is former interim dean of the College of Education. Dr. Wehrman earned his doctorate in counselor education and supervision from the University of South Dakota and his M.S. in applied behavior analysis from St. Cloud State University. Dr. Wehrman is a two-time chair of the National Board for Certified Counselors (NBCC) and Affiliates Board of Directors. Following the 2004 Asian tsunami, he traveled to Sri Lanka to provide psychological first aid to children and to train caregivers and local officials regarding the symptoms of child trauma. Dr. Wehrman is a former medical service officer in the United States military and is a combat veteran. He has received several awards, including a South Dakota Counseling Association Outstanding Service Award and a UCCS Chancellor's award.